Organization Man, Organization Woman: Calling, Leadership, and Culture

ABINGDON PRESS STUDIES IN CHRISTIAN ETHICS
AND ECONOMIC LIFE, VOLUME 4

Organization Man, Organization Woman: Calling, Leadership, and Culture

Shirley J. Roels

With Critical Responses by

Barbara Hilkert Andolsen

and

Paul F. Camenisch

Introduction by

Max L. Stackhouse

Abingdon Press
Nashville

Library of Congress Cataloging-in-Publication Data

Roels, Shirley J.
   Organization man, organization woman: calling, leadership, and culture / Shirley J. Roels; with critical responses by Barbara Hilkert Andolsen and Paul F. Camenisch; introduction by Max L. Stackhouse.
      p.   cm. — (Abingdon Press studies in Christian ethics and economic life; vol. 4)
   Includes bibliographic references.
   ISBN 0-687-00964-2 (alk. paper)
   1. Vocation—Christianity. 2. Christians—Employment. 3. Leadership—Religious aspects—Christianity. 4. Management—Religious aspects—Christianity. 5. Sex role—Religious aspects—Christianity. 6. Sex discrimination in employment. I. Andolsen, Barbara Hilkert. II. Camenisch, Paul F. III. Stackhouse, Max L. IV. Title. V. Series: Abingdon Press studies in Christian ethics and economic life; #4.
   BV4740.R64   1997
   261.8'5—dc21   97-19990
                                                                              CIP

Contents

Preface 7

Introduction
    Max L. Stackhouse 11

Chapter 1: Organization Man; Organization Woman:
    Faith, Gender, and Management
    Shirley J. Roels 17
        Introduction: Faith, Gender, and Organizational Life . . . 17
        Calling: The Divine/Human Connection 22
        Leadership: Human-to-Human Relationships 45
        Culture: Creating the Organizational Ethos 66
        Conclusion: Out to Whatever the Future Holds 78

Chapter 2: Feminist Theological Reflections on Justice
    and Solidarity with Women Workers
    Barbara Hilkert Andolsen 81

Chapter 3: Men and Women in Business: On Professional
    Ethics and the Limits of Theology
    Paul F. Camenisch 97

Chapter 4: In Response
    Shirley J. Roels 119

Notes 129

Contributors 133

Preface

This series is written to aid in the reconstruction of Christian ethics as it bears on economic life in our increasingly global era. Reconstruction is necessary because much of the analysis used by theologians and pastors to think about economic life in the past few decades is socially and theologically suspect.

It was not only political scientists who failed to predict the collapse of Eastern Europe by failing to read the signs of the times. Nor was it only economists who argued for massive loans by private banks to doubtful governments and did not foresee the consequences of these debts. Nor can we say it was only sociologists who denied the evidence of religious resurgence around the world because they believed that modernization would secularize everyone, or only anthropologists who argued that religion is an aspect of culture and every culture's ethic is equal to every other one, or only politicians who began to see all issues only in terms of power analysis. It was not only philosophers and literary critics who began to deconstruct every normative claim. These all contributed to the demoralization of intellectual and religious life, to a vacuity in social ethics; but, it must be said, it was also the theologians and pastors.

In conferences on the implications of the Fall of the Wall sponsored by the Lilly Endowment, one hosted by Trotz Rendtorff in Munich and another by Peter Berger in Boston, it became clear that ideological differences had obscured for many the deeper social and ethical forces that shape modern life, as well as many biblical and theological motifs that are decisive for faith and ethics. It is not the case that no contribution to the future was made in these decades. Some evil was undone; some good was done. Many colonial, racist, and sexist structures were challenged, if not fully banished, and many people were exposed to new possibilities. But many views of what brought these about, and many of the social and theological theories that various advocates of liberation use to guide the present toward the future are thin, false, confused, or perilous. They cannot

7

help us discover the ethical fabric necessary for a global society, or the theological bases by which to discern or construct one.

We are closer to Ezra and Nehemiah (rebuilding the city on the base of the past) or the early church (engaging and reshaping a cosmopolitan culture) than we are to the Exodus, the Conquest, the Apocalypse, or the New Jerusalem. The prophetic task today is to reconstruct social ethics boldly, under insecure and ambiguous conditions, while confessing our sins and seeking to be socially realistic, intellectually cogent, and theologically faithful.

To reform ethics, we offer a series of volumes, exploring the following hypotheses, recognizing that not everyone agrees:

- We face the prospect of a worldwide, multicultural society in which democratic constitutional polities, human rights, ethnic interests, nationalist forces, media images, and corporate capitalist forces will be decisive influences—and sometimes in conflict, needing ethical guidance.

- Economic forces are largely driving these developments and are themselves substantially driven by materialistic motivations, but they are also shaped by and subject to social, cultural, and spiritual influences, even if these are presently confused, inarticulate, or questionable.

- Religion invariably shapes a society's cultural and spiritual values; thus, no area of social life is purely secular, but since religion exists in the midst of social realities, it makes a great deal of difference what religion is present and how it relates to social realities.

- Economic life, as a peculiar mix of calculated interest, socio-political formation, and religio-ethical commitment, stands as a key test as to whether the future will be a blessing or a curse to humanity.

- Theological understandings of the Bible and the classic tradition, in a reconstructive dialogue with the social and human sciences, can correct religious errors, contribute to the understanding of social and economic life, and render a Christian ethic to guide the emerging world civilization.

Such issues will be pursued by the method of "apologetic dialogue." "Apologetics" is often contrasted to "dogmatics" which seeks to set forth the doctrinal teaching of the church on its own terms. Dogmatics has its important place, and will often serve as a resource to our efforts. But apologetics seeks to show when, where, and how Christian faith and ethics are intellectually and morally valid and to engage in critical and mutually corrective dialogue with those who doubt all of it from without or major parts of it from within. Since many do not know of, hold to, or care about dogmatic matters as they bear on social and economic life, we must show the significance of theology in and for public discourse.

We do this in a dialogical setting and for the dialogical settings of teaching and learning. Supported by the Project on Public Theology at Princeton Theological Seminary, funded by the Lilly Endowment and by Abingdon Press, our editorial board meets twice a year for discussion of the matters that appear in print, and each volume will have three or more perspectives on its topic. The board and all contributors are Christian, and all have studied the relationship of Christian ethics to economic life. We come from several backgrounds and traditions—Ecumenical, Evangelical, and Roman Catholic. Most are Protestant. We represent several fields of study. Some positions, however, are not represented. No one is flatly a libertarian, humanist, liberationist, or fundamentalist, although members of our group are convinced that, with proper theological qualification, each of these views could make a contribution to some aspect of our thought together. Taken alone, we believe, each of these views tends to be reductionistic, dishonest, and unfaithful. Yet, we also suspect that each of these views poses a question that must be answered: What preserves individual dignity and freedom? What place ought Christianity to give to humanist values and to the place of humanity in the plenitude of creation? What serves the poor and the oppressed and helps us understand the reasons for their situations? And, what is fundamental in faith and morals?

We are believers seeking to identify the ethics required for economic and social reconstruction, less like those who write party platforms to vent opinion or gain power than those who write briefs in and for a collegium of individuals who are attempting to adjudicate important matters from different angles of view, to plumb deeper, to seek a truer view, and to find a better way for the common life. We invite all who will to join us.

Max L. Stackhouse
General Editor

Already Published

Volume 1: *Christian Social Ethics in a Global Era*
Max L. Stackhouse, with Peter L. Berger,
Dennis P. McCann, and M. Douglas Meeks

Volume 2: *Environmental Ethics and Christian Humanism*
Thomas Sieger Derr, with James A. Nash
and Richard John Neuhaus

Volume 3: *The Business Corporation and Productive Justice*
David A. Krueger, with Donald W. Shriver, Jr.
and Laura L. Nash

Other Volumes to be Announced

Introduction

Max L. Stackhouse

Three dramatic economic changes converge in the contemporary experience of organizational life as women and men experience it today. First, the corporation, whether an incorporated local firm or an international conglomerate, as already discussed in volumes 1 and 3 of this series, has emerged as the primary locus of employment, production, and professional activity for contemporary economic activity. The central economic roles of both the household and the government, the organizers of production, employment, professional roles, and economic distribution in previous eras and in some contemporary underdeveloped and socialist societies, have been displaced by that new organizational reality, the corporation—profit or nonprofit, privately or publicly held. Some who prefer agrarian or small-town life, or prefer strong centralized government, for life-style reasons or because of ecological or social justice theories, as already discussed in volumes 1 and 2 of this series, may be quite disconsolate about this development; but it shows little chance of being altered in the near future. Among other things, it is forcing the reconsideration of the nature and character of the professions, and it is creating new spheres of specialized function, expertise, and responsibility in society that alter the shape of the common life altogether.

Second, women have flooded into the world of these corporations and professions in numbers scarcely imaginable only a generation ago. Women have always worked, but historically much of the labor in the village, on the farm, or even in the Victorian cities, was often home-related, sex-segregated, and much less highly regarded and rewarded than the work of men. Today, with higher levels of education and with more, although not pervasive, acceptance of women as full and equal partners in the corporate workplace, many dynamics of traditional male-female relationships are under scrutiny and revision. Not only are the expectations, habits, and patterns of family life being revised by these changes, but the relative economic independence of women is altering areas of social perception, leadership, and professional behavior in society at large.

Third, the economy, with its global markets in capital, labor, technology, communication, and talent, is having effects that are quite unsettling. Local markets and settled economic practices can easily be swamped and dislocated by these developments. Competition for jobs lowers wages for some and competition for talent raises salaries for others. The technology that brings with it relatively inexpensive transportation, leaves nearby communities vulnerable to long-distant competitors. Those who had a dignified place in previous systems find that they are displaced by methods and practices that have no need of their skills, no place for their obsolete source of dignity. The relative ease with which middle- and upper-class Euro-American women have been able to enter the global future is matched by the difficulties with which less acculturated peoples of color, male or female, face escalating standards of international competition.

Yet, the globalization of the economy has meant opportunity for people previously excluded by nation-state boundaries from protected jobs markets. New middle classes (by world standards, even if they are "upper lower" class standards by the North Atlantic nations) are being created at record speed—with, to be sure, no small amount of turmoil and dislocation in more developed and the previously underdeveloped lands. Whether the globalization of the economy can translate into a global society, or even a global civilization that will be marked by at least degrees of relative justice and equality, broadening and deepening the sense of who the "us" of the common life might be, is very much an open question. Women play distinctive roles in this situation also. For example, it is increasingly well documented that low-interest, relatively small loans to local enterprises, often run by women, are among the fastest ways to bring development to poverty-stricken areas. And it is clear that with increased education and economic opportunity, birth rates tend to decline—lowering the demand on resources by burgeoning populations, and allowing women of child-bearing age to participate more fully in the productivity and rewards of a growing economy. This, in turn, tends to alter residual patterns of male domination, and bring

12

about greater justice in family, economic, and social life generally. For all the problems that remain in the West generally, and in America particularly, the moral values that enhance greater respect for human rights and social equity are now being developed precisely where new professional opportunities in corporate life are the most open to women. In this regard, the West in general, and America in particular, is setting the pace for much of the world. What happens here, in this area, is likely to happen elsewhere, with due respect for the particulars of cultural adaptation and correction for cultural imperialism. In any case, future global standards are more likely to approximate contemporary Western standards of corporate leadership, basic equality between males and females, the development of new areas of professional life, and the increased interdependence of peoples around the world.

If something like the convergence of these three factors is actually the case, we face several major ethical questions. For one thing, it is a major question as to whether we should morally and spiritually embrace this situation, or resist it. It is, after all, morally ambiguous, and it is never simply a matter of identifying the tides of history and floating with them. Human discernments are always morally complicated and interest-laden and it is wise to investigate whether or not we are embracing what ought to be embraced. Should we determine that these directions are unavoidable for the foreseeable future, a related question is whether or not we should attempt to shape them, to revise or reform them, by applying some higher principles or goals. Indeed, we might claim that such directions have themselves been charted by the deeper ethical choices of our ancestors, and are woven into the fabric of present trends by those in previous generations who sought to live by grand principles and purposes and who created a culture which brought about our present tendencies. If this is so, we must ask whether we need to endorse or revise the principles and purposes that guided our forebears, re-invigorate or repudiate the values that they plowed into the moral ecology into which we have been socialized and acculturated.

The question is, of course, from whence come the standards by which we can make moral choices of this order. What are the ethical standards to which we should turn, if we are to oppose, celebrate, or modulate the changes brought about by the convergence of these major transformations in organizational structures, gender roles, and global life?

We can hardly draw our ethical standards from society, for that is what is changing. Nor is it easy to draw them from nature, for at least some aspects of nature are being changed by technology and other aspects of what we thought was "natural" are proving to have been social conventions. The scholars who write in this volume are all Christian. Shirley Roels, the author of the lead essay, is an Evangelical Calvinist; she is a professor of management, an educational administrator, and an organizational consultant to the Christian Reformed Church. Barbara Andolsen, the author of the first critical response, is a Roman Catholic religious feminist. Paul Camenisch, the second critical respondent, is an Ecumenical Presbyterian. The perspectives they present deal not only with distinctive views of corporate life and organizational change, the relationships of males and females in the workplace and in the society at large, and the effects of globalization on these matters, but also with the larger issue of whether or not theology, especially Christian theology, can provide the basic resources for guiding our moral choices in our present situation. In ways that will be surprising to some, the theological issue turns out to be decisive, precisely because it serves as the lens through which not only the ethical issues, but also the sociological, psychological, and geo-economic issues are read. This, of course, is one of the goals of this volume and of this series: to explore the ways in which, and the degree to which, a theologically informed ethic can and should shape our perceptions of, and strategies for dealing with, the dynamic and changing forms of contemporary economic life.

Roels argues, in the lead essay, that major themes from the classic Christian tradition—"vocation," "covenant," "image of God," and "Trinity"—not only can but in some cases must inform the emerging patterns and possibilities in which we today live and move and have our being. She also suggests that these are pertinent to those who are non-Christians, although she is especially addressing those who self-consciously draw on the biblical and doctrinal traditions to find their moral and spiritual rudders.

The fact that women are moving into positions of organizational leadership in the corporations of modern life is, to her theological eye, a step in the direction of God's *shalom*, the "just peace" that comes, finally, only with the fullness of God's reign on earth. While sharply critical of the residual resistance to justice and reconciliation, and fully alert to the persistence of evil and sin between genders, races, nations, and egocentric selves, she basically sees signs of

14

promise in the current developments. Further, she is convinced that the opening of new spheres of differentiated social existence, each with its own particular demand for professional development, is a providential sign of grace for many. And in these areas, she holds that key elements of Christian theological ethics, stripped of their patriarchal distortions, can guide women and men better than any other alternative.

The first critic, Barbara Andolsen, is more ambiguous about exactly these matters. Her attention has for some years been focused on the plight of lower-level workers in contemporary economies, especially on female clerical staff, many of whom come from less privileged backgrounds. They do not so clearly benefit from the new conditions, especially when their situation is interpreted through the U.S. Roman Catholic Bishops Pastoral Letter on the Economy, "Justice for All." Portions of that letter also cohere with her more radical feminist perspective, although some selectivity about the teachings of the bishops and in regard to radical feminism is present in her essay. While not calling for outright resistance to our present directions, it is fair to say that Andolsen is considerably more reserved in her endorsement of them, and her use of some revisionist theological themes which come from one wing of Christian feminism evokes a lively rejoinder from Roels.

The second critic, Paul Camenisch, largely supports the advocacy for women's equal place in the world of work, which both of the previous authors advocate. His major focus, however, is on the basic issue whether organizational management and the other "newer professions" that are appearing in contemporary corporate life are really professions. Tracing some of the classical defining marks of what it means to be a professional, he raises several questions that all claimants to professional status will surely have to face. At a different level, he also poses the question that some Christians and many non-Christians are putting to those who would advocate a Christian theological base for the ethics by which they want to guide behavior in public life. Is it not in fact the case that ideas such as "vocation," "covenant," and "Trinity" are quite specific to a particular religious tradition, and that, in dealing with issues in the common life in a pluralistic society, we cannot expect such ideas to guide public discourse, consensus, or policy in government, corporation, or profession without discrimination against those who do not already share belief in them? While agreeing with Camenisch on many points, Roels thinks that he is mistaken on both of these points, and argues in her rejoinder against his more restricted use of the term "profession" and his view of key theological concepts as pertinent only to "insider" Christian discourse.

Without doubt, women and men are going to encounter one another in the professions and in the public spheres of organizational life for as long as we can imagine, and they will do so on new terms and around the globe. Not only for believers, but for all who are shaped by the effects of an emerging organizational culture that has at least some of its roots in a civilization deeply stamped by centuries of Christian influences, it is likely that our capacity for discovering the morals necessary to guide our lives together will depend in substantial measure on our capacity for wrestling effectively with basic questions that, classically, were framed by theological ethics. The authors in this volume not only draw on the treasures of the past, but offer nuanced appraisals of the present, and force us to face the issues of the future where the effects of feminism and of the secularization of the professions is a fact of life. I tend to agree with Roels that the resources of the classical tradition remain the best guide for a contemporary public theology; but it is only in dialogue with critics such as are represented here that the case for this view can be convincingly made today. Together, these authors offer us a substantial contribution to the future.

Chapter 1

Organization Man, Organization Woman: Faith, Gender, and Management

Shirley J. Roels

Introduction: Faith, Gender, and Organizational Life

Gender relations play a major, but often hidden, role in organizational life. People, of course, note rather early whether their colleagues at work are female or male, friendly or not, and available for non-work exchanges or not. Yet far beyond such immediate impressions, gender-related factors subtly shape attitudes, expectations, and actual performance. Sustained exploration of these factors for global economic life is a relatively recent undertaking. Unfortunately, so is the heightened level of conflict over sex and gender in the workplace.

Both sexuality and the ordering of institutions involve moral issues. Yet contemporary ethics does not answer many of the questions concerning the work of men and women and the relationships of men and women when they work together. Perhaps this occurs because all too frequently we have considered such moral questions as independent of religious faith. Unlike other world population groups, we have treated ethics as separable from fundamental beliefs. In the process we are losing our grip on foundations for understanding the world as God intended it to be. Thus, it is reasonable to take up issues of sexuality in the workplace from a Christian perspective, joining personal faith with reasoned analysis.

Indeed, a thoughtful Christian view of these matters can move us beyond both ponderous treatises and trendy self-help advice. Academic journals and the popular press enhance modes of argu-

17

mentation or illustrate popular sentiment; but often they provide only limited guidance for real life. Besides, scholarly analyses of the sex-based differences are heavily dependent on fears about political correctness, differing interpretations of gender-related statistics, and the value frameworks behind the research.[1] Trendy pop journalists create images of work and family living which frequently fail to correspond with reality, and glib books on managerial improvement constitute a cottage industry. Everyone from Mary Kay Ash to Zig Ziglar recognizes the ready audience for tips, biographies, and self-help guides which purport to carve the female or male path to success. The viability of such resources is arguably evidence of a craving for moral wisdom grounded in faith and connected to life.

A faith-based analysis may also help the church move beyond the impasse in its thinking about managerial life, an area in which many churches have provided little help to the faithful. Some church leaders, attracted to Christian socialism, still harbored deep suspicions of anyone in managerial life. They prefer to talk only about macroeconomic structures, while holding the business world of their parishioners at an arm's length. Other church leaders embrace "Christian capitalism" but do not lead their congregations in sorting through the complexities of contemporary economic life.

For the most part the "info-hype" which circulates in books, TV talk shows, and news magazines along with Sunday morning judgments on economic systems only leave us confused. As a result our descriptions of human sexuality, organizational excellence, and career success are often secular and nearly always devoid of theology— subtly, of course—since we simply have not created a place for thoughtful consideration of God. The conflicts that result from these discussions create a cultural minefield as we ponder profound shifts that are radically altering the work lives of both men and women. We rightly wonder what God requires of humanity as we undertake vocations that will shape organizations and social life in the twenty-first century. If we truly desire to discern God's norms and purposes for this world, how do we find the intersection of God's will, our work as men and women interacting in complex organizations, and the choices we make affecting the lives of countless others with whom we work?

Besides, we now live in an "on-line" global network of organizations, and the patterns of organizational interaction we create are quickly exported. Our cultural treatments affect men and women of other societies at least as much as we adopt and adapt insights that their cultures provide. The re-blending of faith, gender, and organizational life extends far beyond North America, and we surely have a duty to export ideas and models which are as just and right as we can discern and develop.

This is not the world of our parents. In the changing ganglia of organizational cultures we make decisions each day, often without the benefit of hindsight or conscious foresight about how we daily serve the living Creator of the universe and lead our Creator's world into the next millennium, from what is to what ought to be. With few predecessors having faced what we face, and with limited help from the sciences, we need more than ever a public theology about gender in organizational life.

We need a public theology to guide our choice making and our leadership, a theology that digs beyond guides to personal success and asks about our God-given responsibilities as men and women as we work together in a new environment. I shall argue that we need a Christian understanding of the intersection of gender and responsibility in organizational life, which can be a source of motivation, challenge, and even delight, a theology beyond the shelter of the church, a theology for the world of work.

Some may wonder whether this book is written for them. They cannot imagine a reasonable discussion about the intersection of gender concerns, Christian faith, and professional work in a market economy. Men and women outside the Christian faith may question the relevance of such faith to an effective market economy. Some may grant that religion affects values, and perhaps values indirectly shape market activity; however, they believe in an economy principally based on rational economic behavior, not on allegiance to a specific religion or theological perspective.

Those who embrace Christian faith may be equally skeptical about this argument. Some Christians will be suspicious simply because the analysis focuses on gender. They are suspicious of any commentary that mixes the study of gender with classical Christian theology. As some may see it, gender-based analysis is feminist claptrap; and feminism is perceived as anti-family, anti-faith, and anti-community. These Christians raise questions about feminist-associated ideas, which emphasize freedom instead of accountability; secular relativism instead of absolute Christian values; a message of women's liberation and self-actualization instead of responsibility

19

and service. I will argue that both these concerns have valid elements, but that neither can provide a workable framework for common life in the future. These narrow perspectives must be broadened.

Other Christians will question the need for this analysis because they believe the primary question, namely the service of women in ecclesiastical office, has been settled or is at least on its way to settlement in a host of Christian circles. Thus, they conclude that women now have access to a full range of professional opportunities, including Christian ministries. Since the central crisis has been handled, Christian living can now proceed without continued angst. But, we will see, many questions are quite unsettled. For example, some female Christians, who embrace a selective feminism, may struggle with this book. They may have sifted through feminist ideas to find those with which they feel comfortable as Christians. Such women have learned to understand and value the distinction between "justice feminism" (the moral quest for social/legal equity) and "protest feminism" (the hostile reaction to patriarchy or even to men). However, rarely have they connected their feminist thinking with management concepts. Leaders of profit and not-for-profit organizations lean heavily on organizational theory as it has been most deeply developed within Western market capitalism. By contrast, the language and thought constructs of much feminism have borrowed heavily from the Marxist tradition. In a framework emphasizing oppression and class struggle, these women, though Christian, see organizations within the market economy, particularly the for-profit variety, as tools of domination. In their minds they believe the market economy *inherently* suppresses the drive for gender equality. The status of women in proletarian secretarial roles and men in bourgeois management roles is proof positive of capitalism's inherent evil!

Other readers may focus most on their puzzlement. Male Christians may believe that gender in the workplace is a topic of concern primarily for aspiring women and need not be one of their primary foci. In their thinking, it's tough for men to figure out what women really want, as past male and female role definitions continue to break down. They perceive women as confused about the intersection of Christian faith, feminist ideas, and a market economy. Do women really aspire to the life of leisure, power, or status without hard work, or to the construction of a lasting organizational contribution? Their resulting strategy is a hands-off one. Let working women privately sort out their aspirations; then provide access for those who decide to continue in the organization if they're qualified, want professional careers, and can arrange a corporate fit. Many Christian men are not convinced that the matter of gender needs much attention.

Finally, Christian women and men who work in blue or pink collar occupations or in developing economies may question the general relevance of a book about faith, gender, and organizational life. In the day-to-day struggles of their lives they wonder about any possible benefit from a discussion about gender relations and leadership in organizations. The men and women they know work in paid employment simply to support their families. How can they benefit from a more theological struggle over gender within the upper echelons of organizational life?

For many different reasons, the groups cited above suggest that gender relations in the workplace should not be a matter of serious theological and organizational concern. However, I believe otherwise, and I hope to assist each of the above groups in developing deeper faith-based understandings of managerial calling, leadership requirements, and organizational culture, while simultaneously grappling with gender concerns.

We can approach the issues by sifting through the subtleties of the cultural shifts in gender relations, and then asking what it takes to effectively negotiate this shift for ourselves while mediating the struggle for others in our organizations. And, we do this with the conviction that our Creator shaped us as choice-making, sex-differentiated creatures for whom work is a central part of human life. Yet work for both men and women has been substantially redefined in the last half of the twentieth century.

What has changed? The economic competition; the advent of new technologies; changing gender roles in society; and the emergence of the professionally educated manager as a leader in the organizational world. If we desire Christian faith to be integrated into this profoundly complex and ever changing work environment, we must rethink our responsibilities as working men and women in organizations approaching the twenty-first century.

Most adults, both female and male, will spend at least thirty-five to forty years in the paid labor force. Particularly for women, participation in the paid labor force has risen steadily since 1900. Even when adults leave paid employment to tend to their small children, this is only a short break, often less than ten years, from paid work. The challenge of finding our way as men and women working together in paid employment will affect us all in the twenty-first century, and managers influenced by Christianity will be among those expected to chart paths into the future.

This essay, then, is for all called to explore paths to tomorrow in this changing time, in a world where Christian theology, social structure, professional experience, global change, and serious aspiration do not always mesh. It is intended as a sustained exploration of possible paths through the tangle of messages we receive from media, mailboxes, faxes, friends, and family. It suggests that Christian theology can help us through the maze when biological, psychological, educational, sociological, political, economic, and theological factors all mix together, and we are constrained by imperfect information and limited rationality. It intends to help us lead balanced lives which honor our families, churches, neighborhoods, schools, and communities as well as ourselves in paid employment. Indeed, it suggests that we will best find our way when our lives are deeply grounded in identity with and service to the true God.

Calling: The Divine/Human Connection

In the late twentieth century, females and males of all religious faiths seek careers as professional managers. No matter what the concept of the divine, human conceptions of ultimate reality shape aspirations and actions. Ideas, or the lack of them, about the divine/human connection also affect the values by which people shape their organizational cultures. Sometimes the beliefs of professional managers radiate beyond particular organizations to shape perspectives and policies throughout the world.

Within this mix, Christian thinking can contribute a special perspective to organizational life and the actions of men and women working as managerial professionals. Christians bring particular concepts of the divine/human relationship to their workplaces and shape how they think and how act. However, such perspectives sometimes need further development to connect matters of gender with organizational life and leadership. Christians have had limited influence in this regard because our knowledge about the nature of managerial work in a global market economy is sketchy. We may also be confused about the differences between "sex" and "gender," or we may not know how human identity, from a Christian viewpoint, ought to be connected with professional work as managers.

The Professionalization of Management

Most managers choose their line of work. Many of them could have become lawyers, doctors, pastors, scientists, teachers, members of professions that have existed for hundreds of years. Instead, upon examining their talents, some men and women have chosen, or been chosen by organizations, to link their identities with a type of employment that has come to be called "professional" only in the late twentieth century.

The idea of management has existed since ancient times. All that we know of Egypt, Babylon, China, and India suggests that some leaders knew how to manage rather large groups of people, and we can hardly imagine the biblical stories without thinking about management. Noah must have needed excellent management skills to complete the ark. Abraham must have managed his flocks, herds, and household well to accomplish the journey from Ur to Canaan. In Exodus, Moses listened when his father-in-law Jethro recommend an organizational structure that could simultaneously manage Israel's disputes and avoid leader burnout. In Judges, Deborah's leadership motivated Barak's army to overcome the Canaanites. No doubt all of these Old Testament leaders had management gifts.

Yet it is hardly likely that the biblical ancients viewed themselves as professional managers. Instead, they saw themselves as people with religious callings. By contrast, our understanding of professional management is much less connected with religious faith and much more connected to contemporary social changes, the emergence and growth of twentieth century forms of organization, and a mid-century revolution in the nature of Western managerial education. Without these changes there would be no sense of management as the global profession we now understand it to be. However, in the process we have lost a sense of management as a religious calling, equally open to both males and females. How did this happen and what have been the implications of this loss?

Preindustrial cottage industries had space for the organizing efforts of both men and women even if there were typical areas of responsibility. Frequently women produced items such as clothing, candles, food, and household goods while men crafted items of leather, wood, and metal. However, the shift to industrialized factory labor required physical strength and endurance. It removed the worker from the household and from the care of children, changing the female/male balance of the cottage industries. This nineteenth-century change in the structure of production sent economic culture-building activities down a new road, as production and distribution were removed from the household.

Still, throughout that century, management was not a profession but a job and a community role, one principally occupied by males. Organizations in the United States were much smaller and locally focused. Towns had their grocers, barbers, dressmakers, and blacksmiths. Most organizational activity was conducted in the context of particular communities. Early manufacturers and shop owners intersected with their immediate neighbors on a daily basis. They likely worried most about enough income to feed their families and the families of just a few employees. While managers needed to work hard, the level of conceptual skill needed to be an effective manager did not require an advanced or specialized education beyond basic reading, writing, and arithmetic to aid the craft or trade skill. The management foundation was "how to do," not "how to think," and businessmen prided themselves on being good doers.

Large-scale business corporations emerged in the late nineteenth century as the railroad and telegraph lines allowed for national markets. Yet management still was not seen as a profession. Instead, business enterprises were frequently created by male entrepreneurs possessing the financial capital to dominate an industry. The Rockefellers and the Vanderbilts were seen, not as managerial professionals, but as powerful men ruling closely owned corporations. While many admired Henry Ford's drive to manufacture the affordable middle-class car, there was no doubt about who ran the Ford corporate enterprise! Early-twentieth-century owners were also the company managers. Thus, the focus was on the ownership of the business, not on the administrative talent of nonowners.

The profession of management emerges when the separation between ownership and management becomes more distinct in the second half of twentieth-century U.S. history. As corporate enterprises grew, the range of institutional and individual investors expanded, and differentiation between owners and managers grew, due to the increased use of stocks and bonds. On the brink of the

24

twenty-first century, the global economy is no longer based principally on the owner/manager paradigm. Instead, stock is frequently held by life insurance companies, pension funds, and brokerage house portfolios, and is invested for clients who are at least a couple of managerial steps removed from the businesses themselves. Professional global managers, albeit having some stock or options in their companies as a portion of compensation, trot the globe representing large public enterprises and introducing a new sense of the word "public," one quite distinct from national governments. The tight link between ownership and management, characteristic of the first part of this century, has broken down. With that breakdown there is now as much focus on the professional managers who run the businesses as on those who hold the stock. Mental frameworks for the future, strategic analyses of the present, and shrewd understandings of industrial development have become the intellectual capital that professional managers use to create wealth for disparate groups of shareholders.

The emergence of management as a profession was aided by shifts in the nature of managerial education. Business schools, even into the 1950s, maintained a "how to do" strategy in educating those who would become organizational managers, a strategy not usually associated with the professions. However, the 1959 Gordon-Howell and Pierson reports on business education[2] were the catalysts for changing the underlying paradigm of management education. These reports argued for business education that was much more conceptually grounded, particularly in the social sciences. Managers must first and foremost learn "how to think" about organizational problems. Given the expanding knowledge base about economic systems and organizational behavior, learning "how to think" effectively about management would require extended education, perhaps even an M.B.A. degree. With this new focus on studying a systematic body of knowledge and learning analytical skills related to administration, management was gradually given more credence as a profession. It now fit more closely the pattern of other occupations classified as professions, in which a liberal arts education was coupled to applied knowledge of the field.

Furthermore, some schools believed that their new, more conceptual approach to business problems could also be used in not-for-profit entities. Organizations, be they profit or not-for-profit, needed to plan, organize, motivate, and control. Both needed to attract, select, train, and develop employees. Both needed to organize financial and physical resources. By the mid- to late-1970s professional managers were beginning to emerge as leaders in not-for-profit organizations as well. The trend to employ professional managers in hospitals, social services, schools, and even the arts continues.

Now, as the end of the century approaches, the distinctly American approach to managerial education is spreading internationally. Universities within countries experiencing the transition to a market economy are scrambling to develop Western-style professional programs in business education at both undergraduate and graduate levels. As corporations and managerial education have been modified over the course of the twentieth century, and as state-controlled economies continue to wither, the work of managers in both profit and not-for-profit settings continues to be built into a distinct global profession.

The transition of management from a how-to-do trade to a how-to-think profession made it more accessible and intriguing for females. The managerial profession is now based less on physical strength or the financial capital for business ownership, areas in which many women would be disadvantaged. Conceptual ability, where women have no obvious disadvantage, is the foundation. Managerial education can now be part of women's normal progression through the college systems of the Western world. Such education can also build on the organizational experiences of women in a variety of not-for-profit settings, a traditional stronghold for both paid and volunteer women. The revolution in the managerial profession created a synergistic fit with the revolution in gender roles simultaneously underway in the United States; and because the United States' system of managerial education is now being exported around the globe, the signals carried about appropriate roles for men and women will go with this system into other cultures. It is in this context that gender becomes a variable affecting the managerial profession and a factor to be managed in the workplace.

Gender and the Managerial Profession

The managerial profession matured in the United States during the same decades in which gender roles were being redefined in American society. The culture and the standards for operation of professions existing since medieval times were much more settled;

but the managerial profession has been maturing within the caul-dron of American social change. Thus, the management profession has been profoundly affected by the shifting of gender roles over the past few decades. What real effects have resulted from the intersec-tion of these changes?

One of the landmark books of the era, *The American Business Creed*, documented the public stance of businessmen concerning business purposes and culture shortly after World War II.[3] This informal creed espoused faith in rational economic structures manip-ulable for human betterment and the business occupation as a some-what Puritan calling. However, the creed also presumed a group of people existed who would commit themselves to this type of work despite its average occupational status. The presumption was that men would trade the lower occupational status of business for its higher income and social status. Many men in the decade that followed did exactly that.

William H. Whyte, Jr., in his famous 1956 book *The Organization Man*, portrayed the life of male corporate managers.[4] The picture was one of men who sold their souls to the corporate enterprise, typically to one corporation for their working lives. Their first loyalties were to the corporation, which controlled their career progress. When the corporation said "move to California," they did; and when, perhaps only two years later, the corporation said "move to Connecticut," they did. Their social lives and the lives of their families were bound up with their companies. These men worked long hours, while their wives raised the children, managed the social calendars, and in-vested themselves in supporting their husband's careers. The corpo-ration was seen not only as a source of family income, but also as a primary source of family identity and social status.

Yet by 1963, just seven years later, Betty Friedan was writing in *The Feminine Mystique* about the problem of the women who were married to these men. She identified it as "the problem which has no name."[5] Friedan describes the boredom of housework, the anomie of rootless suburbs, and the drifting sense of purposelessness felt by women whose days were consumed by car pools, the tennis club, vacuumed perfection, and the creation of appealing food for innu-merable corporate socials. Her book challenged women to look at their talents and the sources of their identity in a search for different lives.

The challenge of such women writers by the early 1970s spurred

women to consider alternative futures. While some, where permit-
ted, entered the time-honored professions of law, medicine, and
theology, others choose to study management and enter the ranks of
this fluid, still emerging profession. Margaret Hennig and Anne
Jardim, in their 1973 book *The Managerial Woman*, caused a national
stir by documenting the experiences of the early women pioneers in
the professional management culture.[6] Based on their doctoral research while at Harvard Business School, these authors described the
attributes which led some women into management careers; however, they also described the maleness of the managerial culture and
the challenge for new women managers who were just beginning to
struggle in this culture. While Hennig and Jardim supported legislation to open opportunities for women, they placed a stronger emphasis on understanding male and female beliefs, attitudes, and
assumptions in the workplace, ideas which could build or destroy
the abilities of men and women to work together.

In 1977 Rosabeth Moss Kanter's *Men and Women of the Corporation*
looked again at the landscape that William H. Whyte had described
only two decades earlier.[7] His original portrait was being repainted.
It was no longer a picture of male managers at work with wives at
home. Instead, Kanter's image was one of men and women at work
together, albeit not equally. Women's progress through the organizational ranks was uneven. Some women had been isolated in staff
functions that did not provide a foundation for further development.
Others who became pregnant found it difficult to reconcile inflexible
managerial schedules with the demands of motherhood.

While women struggled to find their stride in predominantly
male organizational cultures, men were equally perplexed about
how to treat these relatively new arrivals in the managerial ranks.
Particularly at senior levels of management, women were few and
far between. Those who did thrive on the managerial scene did not
easily fit the picture. Kanter's study documented the difficulty of
incorporating the "different one" at senior levels of management
where hard choices had to be made and environmental uncertainty
was high. At that level, a comfortable consensus about direction was
more easily achieved when all the viewpoints were shared by those
who had the common culture of, say, the locker room. The phrase,
"Why can't a woman be more like a man?" was undoubtedly used
by more than one exasperated male manager.

Yet, in twenty years a profound change in the nature of the

managerial profession had occurred. Managerial work, which had been almost exclusively male since its inception in the United States, was now a profession, and one increasingly populated by both females and males.

Such social changes are never easy. Men, despite acknowledging some sad results of the 1950s organizational culture, still struggle to understand and accommodate women, who do not fit that earlier paradigm of corporate culture and its related societal structure. Women still struggle to find career success while balancing marriage and family, community, and friendships, and wanting to preserve some treasured values from women's experience in more traditional roles. Corporations are at many different points on the continuum of accommodating these changes; and some continue to wonder whether for women, particularly married women with children, "breaking the glass ceiling" into senior management ranks is possible and beneficial.

Finally, the framework for managerial careers is being over-hauled as corporate structures are re-engineered and "right-sized," as the home office comes on-line, as technology creates new pioneers and power bases. When the dominant frames for the future are decentralization, customization, multiple work rhythms, and rapid response; when economic globalization creates strategic upheaval; and when leadership is more akin to orchestrating a jazz band than commanding an army, consciously crafted corporate change affects all men and women who manage.

Management as a profession is still young. It was conceived as an American male but it is developing into global children of both sexes. It is no wonder that in this tumultuous environment both male and female managers struggle to find their way. Like Alice in Wonderland both of them must ask, "Would you tell me, please, which way I ought to go from here?"; and both are frustrated by the Cheshire cat's answer, "That depends a good deal on where you want to get to."[8]

In this fluid, uncertain context managerial men and women struggle to find their professional voices. Professional and personal identity are intertwined. Managerial work is the source of income but also of social connectedness. Through such work roles we build national and international affiliations, connect with a variety of public policies, and find our sense of cultural influence in a multicultural environment. For many of us, managerial work is crucial to who we are and vital in our quest to reshape some small part of the world. Yet, even if we thrive on the chaos, too many of us have left God behind. With no center, we will be pulled apart.

To find our way over the tumult, managers, both female and male, need to think more theologically about their chosen occupation and their future organizational leadership. Over the past few decades both females and males have allowed themselves to be led astray in understanding their professional managerial roles, making fundamental mistakes about their own identities and the relationship of these identities to paid managerial employment.

The first fundamental mistake is the naturalist error of assuming that sexual differences should be foremost in determining human identity and the professional lives that grow from that identity. The second fundamental mistake is the secularist error of assuming that career identity equals full vocational identity. Both of these views, widely held in society, block our access to a deeper theological view of vocation that is important for women and men called to positions of managerial leadership.

Sexual Identity and Human Identity

If we assume that gender should be the foremost determinant of human identity, the struggle over "right" roles for men and women in organizational life becomes central and monumental. On the one hand, consider Ryan Winter, a fictional sales manager. He presumes that male/female differences cast men and women in particular societal roles, men as breadwinners and women as caretakers. Thus, he is uncomfortable with the entry of women into the managerial ranks. Ryan prefers corporations to be male dominated, believing that's the way life should be structured. When women are employed, he expects them to occupy lesser roles in organizations or eventually leave because of family responsibilities. He's quite content to let women work as clerks in customer service but can't imagine one of them as a marketing manager, particularly *his* marketing manager. Ryan is determined that his organization should not change to accommodate more professional women because the right role for men is economic and the right role for women is nurturing. For him, the competitive struggle in the business organization is critical to being a responsible member of society. Ryan believes God intended women principally as "helpmeets" for men and commanded females to "be fruitful and multiply."

On the other hand, consider Kate Summer, a fictional company recruiter. She believes that male/female differences in identity inherently give each sex special insight and talent. She argues that each sex has particular organizational strengths that should be utilized. On that basis she wishes to vary employment opportunities for both sexes. Women should be welcomed into the manufacturing end of the company because they will be nurturing managers, will prove good at details, or will add social polish to the organization. Male managers should be welcomed into the human resources office because they will bring some good financial sense, some analytical thinking, or some closure to ongoing female-dominated discussions among the secretaries.

Whether Ryan Winter and Kate Summer belong to churches or not, their views are essentially naturalistic. Both assume that identity rests first of all in female/male differences. Both managers categorize men and women by their sex and presume that this is the predominant characteristic that makes men or women act as they do.

Such blanket categorizations are dangerous because they run roughshod over individual differences in both men and women. Each man or woman is the product of a highly complex physiology and social background. We cannot make presumptions about particular skills and interests, or the particular lack thereof, on the basis of biological sex, first of all.

In fact, both of these managers are confused about sex and gender. They think they can rightly make presumptions about interests, skills, goals, and social roles on the basis of differences in sexual biology. However, biologically, the number of similarities is far greater than the number of differences between men and women. These managers are not really thinking specifically about biological differences. Instead the real basis for their decisions is an understanding of "gender," cultural categorizations of acceptable styles and roles assigned to men as men and women as women. Both Ryan Winter and Kate Summer are making decisions based on their belief that certain differences in sexual biology, "natural" characteristics, are tightly linked to cultural roles that determine appropriate jobs for men and women. Using such ideas about sexual identity to categorize people blinds them to the uniqueness of each created person, a uniqueness which ought to be honored in organizational life.

Even more foundationally, a nuanced Christian viewpoint would note that, while sexual differences are part of being human, they should not be the primary foundation for our identity at work, anymore than they are in baptism or the voting booth. Christian theology, properly understood, does not hold that biology is destiny, that differences in sexual biology should determine all social roles. Instead, the root of a person's working identity should be each human's relationship to the living God. Our full humanity is realized only in relationship to this God, the One who said, "Let us make humankind in our image, according to our likeness" (Gen. 1:26).

Genesis 1 emphasizes the responsibilities of each human to be a steward and agent for God. The emphasis is not first on sexual distinctions as the basis for a relationship with God. *Adam*, the Hebrew term used, is not a sexually differentiated word. Most likely, *adam* means "person" or "earth creature," encompassing all humankind.[9] Genesis 1 emphasizes the purposes of God and the divine/human interaction that develops out of God's choice to create humankind, not sexual differences, as the first and foremost factor defining this relationship. An intimate relationship between the Divine One and the human one is the first building block of human life. *All* human ones, both male and female, are created to rule as God's trustees in the creation; the human distinction of "man" and "woman" is a secondary one, made to allow for human love and generativity.

Furthermore, in redemption, the New Testament emphasizes the opportunity for males and females to participate equally in the gift of Christ Jesus, not because of their sex, but because of salvation for *human beings*. As Paul so elegantly writes in Galatians 3:27-28, "As many of you as were baptized into Christ have clothed yourselves with Christ. There is no longer Jew or Greek, there is no longer slave or free, there is no longer male and female; for all of you are one in Christ Jesus."

Thus, the very basic Christian theological understanding of the human relationship to God is not, first of all, a story about sexual distinctiveness. It is a story about the God who is beyond gender. It is a story about the great "I Am," the everlasting, dynamic Being who, though separate from us, is always with us. It is the story about a Being that we cannot create or become, who is passionate about both care and justice. It is the story of the true God who is so intimately interested in humans that the only real Son of God died to rescue

God's human creatures, to restore the possibility of faithful service to the Creator, and to insure that our work to transform this world is not in vain.

When we embrace these realities of faith, our first and foremost identity at work and our presumptions about the identity of others in the workplace should not be based on sex or cultural interpretations of gender. The lenses through which we see ourselves and others must shift. Our responsibilities as *humans* are the tie between the unique talents given to each creature and the profound obligations of service to a Redeeming God who has restored our lives. Our work now flows from two sources. One source is gratitude for salvation offered to us through God's grace. The second source is our continuing responsibility to be God's agents as we move toward the kingdom over which God will reign at the endtime. Human gratitude and responsibility should be the sources of our identity at work, and they are not primarily based on our sex.

As a result, we are seriously mistaken when we tie any man or woman to a role in society for which their God-given talents and sense of appropriate service in Creation are ill-matched simply because they are male or female. The standard for our choices and contribution should, first of all, be the individual endowments given by God and the opportunities to use them in God's service. This standard provides the basis for a quest that takes each of us, as individuals, into realms, cultures, and circumstances that we may never have envisioned at earlier points in our lives. We are first and foremost humans in relationship to God and, however important to us, only secondarily male and female in this divine connection. Individual humans are the creational foundation, not males and females grouped by sex.

This foundation provides us with exceptional freedom to explore and pursue many different avenues of human engagement and opportunity for both men and women in organizational work. We should not be bound primarily by the gender-differentiated roles approved in our society. It is our Christian responsibility to transcend gender-based societal structures in our quest to do God's will and find God's desire for others in the workplace. We must deal with human interests, needs, and potential to develop by looking at the particularities of each individual.

However, it does not follow from a Christian framework that those involved in management should *never* use sex and gender as lenses through which we understand our workplace identities or the participation and development of others in the work environment. *Human-to-human* relationships were differentiated by God's choice in Creation as a source of companionship, delight and, of course, procreation. While most of Genesis 1 defines the human purpose for existence, in Genesis 1:28 God charges humans to "be fruitful and multiply, and fill the earth" as well as to "subdue it." Responsibilities for procreation as well as dominion were given to both men and women.

Furthermore, Genesis 2 emphasizes gender differentiation even more clearly. The Hebrew words identifying humans are different than in chapter one. Here, describing the creation of woman in relation to man, the words for human beings are no longer the gender neutral *adam*. Instead the male is named *ish* and the female is identified as *isha*.[10] In Genesis 2 the focus is on the relationship of human beings to each other. Adam and Eve needed human companionship in their work for God as well as their responsibility for multiplying humanity, and a careful reading of the text shows that both males and females were indeed held responsible for the development and protection of the human family. The scenario, therefore, paints a picture of males and females bound together: both are connected to God as human beings; both have responsibilities for management of the world; and both have responsibility for the human family.

However, in Genesis 3 humans introduce sin into the world, and like everything else, female/male relations became troubled. Because of the Fall, humanity has everywhere had family struggles peculiar to the understanding of gender. Still today, relations within our organizations are just as profoundly distorted by the effects of sin.

Sin clouds our understanding of the relative responsibility that organizations should take because of sexually differentiated biology. We do not have perfect answers about how the biological role in child bearing ought to inform our understanding about the rest of women's dominion responsibilities; thus, we are frequently confused about the relative balance of paid employment and family responsibilities for women. Furthermore, we often dismiss the responsibilities for the family that should be also assigned to men, even organizational men.

Sin encourages stereotyping only on the basis of sexual differences. It prevents us from seeing people as unique individuals in whom differences also arise from sources such as race, class, region, and theology. The perspective of a black Presbyterian business-woman in New York may be very different from that of a white Baptist businessman in Oklahoma. The viewpoint of a Catholic businesswoman in Hong Kong and a Pentecostal businessman in Rio de Janeiro will vary; and not primarily because they are female and male! Their frameworks for faith, family life, occupational roles, and future commitments have been shaped by a host of different experiences. Sin makes us all too often content, quite willing to sidestep all of these other factors in organizational life.

The appropriate distribution of organizational power between men and women can also be undercut by sin. One author has posited that perhaps because of the Fall, women are prone to excessive dependency on others for identity and shrink from exercising their proper dominion responsibilities, while men are prone to excessive independence and turn dominion to domination.[11] Perhaps these distortions are the roots of sexual harassment, although knowing that would not excuse its sinful character. Yet these are not the only difficulties we face in organizational life: we also live with cases of passive-dependent males and overly aggressive females who also distort cooperative efforts.

Even more, sin affects the structure of occupations in pernicious ways. Women are typically more clustered in lower-paying jobs than men, and that clustering cannot always be explained by labor supply and demand factors or longevity in the workforce. Around the globe, when women enter higher-paying male job categories, the job categories themselves begin to be transformed. The more these occupations are dominated by females, the less are status and prestige associated with them. There is also evidence that the entry of significant numbers of women into an occupation can even accelerate the exit of males from that job type.

This is where we really live, in a world of fallen structures and relationships, and it very well may take a theological perspective to see this world realistically. We can neither ignore gender-based differences as factors in the work environment nor see them as the only factor in contemporary managerial life. There are just too many aspects of organizational life which are effected.

In summary, it is a mistake to argue that identity in the workplace ought, first of all, to be a matter of gender. Identity should be a matter of relationship between each of us as human beings and the "I Am" who made us and continues to call us each day. Identity ought to be a matter of religious faith above all else. This theological understanding of identity opens up the whole world to each of us, either female or male, as the realm of our potential responsibility. It is the unique combination of talents, calling, and experiences that equips each of us to find our special responsibilities on this earth, responsibilities that will lead us into a variety of challenges in organizational life. It is our responsibility, male or female, to assist others, be they female or male, in establishing the link between an identity grounded in faith and the challenges of organizational life.

Such a Christian stance allows us to acknowledge sex and gender differences that do affect human choices and our organizational cultures. Differences in the sexes were part of original creation but, sadly, have been corrupted by the Fall into sin. However, carefully thinking through Christian theology can prevent the damage caused when identity is defined primarily on the basis of gender.

Professional Identity and Human Identity

Unfortunately, a second mistake, equating personal identity with career, what some call "professional" identity, can be equally damaging to a Christian perspective. Like many secularists we often believe that our professional identities are the most important foundation for who we are and who we will become. William Foote Whyte's managerial men of the 1950s fell into this trap, and women have followed them since the 1970s. Women can idolize paid professional employment and allow it to consume them as it has already consumed many men. The result is often a workaholic life cut off from families, local communities, church life, and personal growth. This secularist viewpoint presumes that the "seculum," the world of the temporal, a world without spiritual significance, should dominate identity. Role or income becomes worth. A multitude of forces still drives us, as men and women managers, to seek our identities principally or exclusively in paid employment. What are these forces?

Many of these factors are the same drives operative in other professional careers. They are inherent in conceptually based work. Conceptual work, tied to a high level of education and training, requires significant planning and commitment of energy for entry into the profession. Managers must also invest substantially in their continuing development. They expect to grow intellectually and emotionally through the challenges of such work. Furthermore, conceptual work goes home in the brain of the manager. There are few boundaries on the time of its performance; it does not stay on the office shelf overnight.

Managerial work also requires the exercise of independent judgment regarding the offering of products or services, the allocation of resources, and care for the people involved in the operation. Thus, an aspiring manager must determine whether he or she possesses the fortitude and willingness to shoulder significant responsibilities.

Because of the investment of educational energy, the willingness to bear responsibility, and the ongoing problem-solving nature of management, such work requires a significant personal investment to be effective. It would be very difficult for managers to tell themselves that the amount of effort expended to achieve a managerial job and the amount of time expended in it don't have a central role in their lives.

A professional position also establishes one's public position and credibility. Managerial work is often the primary launching pad for the rest of a manager's social configuration. Typically, well-paid professional managers, particularly in for-profit environments, have enough income for a broad array of housing options and social experiences. A managerial position also provides the network for involvement in the broader society. Managers may be involved in professional and trade associations, governmental influence groups, community power networks, international linkages, or other business's boards of directors. When one's profession establishes one's public position, it is not easy to discount it as the most important source of life influence.

Other forces that drive the merger of personal and professional identity are unique to the management profession itself. One of these forces is the social science theory underlying management. The other is the effect of the frequent geographic relocation required in many corporate organizations.

Some management theories contribute to the difficulties because of their unconscious allegiance to human self-actualization, implicit in their models of human motivation. For example, Abraham Maslow's hierarchy of needs posits five levels of need, each of which can be tied to workplace sources of motivation. The lowest level, physiological needs, is satisfied at work by acceptable working conditions and base pay which can provide for food and shelter. Above it on the hierarchy, from bottom to top, are the need for safety, belongingness, self-esteem, and finally self-actualization. In Maslow's model this last and highest level need is the one that organizations fulfill through opportunities for training, advancement, and professional growth; but not infrequently the whole scheme is used as a paradigm for motivation at work.

Frederick Herzberg's two-factor theory of motivation has similar overtones. He argues that only the "motivators," namely achievement, recognition, responsibility, the work itself, and personal growth lead to strong job satisfaction and performance. Other factors, labeled "hygiene" items, namely compensation, interpersonal relations, and working conditions, only prevent dissatisfaction. In his theory they will not lead to strong job performance. This theory, too, sometimes blots other dimensions of life out of the range of vision.

Maslow and Herzberg may have intended their work to be descriptive, but their theories are used prescriptively for organizational life. Within their proper scope, such theories have assisted organizations in structuring rewards for employees more effectively. However, managers, in particular, have come to believe that their paid employment ought to be the foremost source of self-actualization, achievement, and recognition as posited by such theories. Since these needs rank highest on the theoretical hierarchies, managers expect such needs to be fulfilled at work. They want such expectations to be met through opportunities to create strategy, control products, make financial decisions, or show community goodwill. While, in themselves, these activities are often good ones, the difficulty lies in the presumption that paid employment is the principle route to self-actualization and personal fulfillment. Fulfilling these needs is then seen as the highest goal for living. There is little distinction between the personal and the professional when one's greatest goals can be accomplished through paid employment. Why not focus the bulk of one's energies there?

We are easily tempted to merge all aspects of community, social, and personal with professional identity but such a quest for fulfillment turns out to be thin and unsatisfying. The biblical understanding is wiser: humans are fulfilled, not principally by actualizing the self, but by intimate connections with God and neighbors in a variety of covenantal bonds including but not limited to the workplace. Thoughtful Christian theology places higher priority on love and justice than on self-actualization alone.

The second factor that differentiates the managerial profession from professions such as law and medicine is frequent geographic relocation of its members. Professional managers in large corporations still move frequently. Local community ties with neighborhoods, churches, and schools are often temporary. Continuity in one's life is through the people with whom one works in an organization or through those whom one meets in other organizations sharing the same specialization. Without strong local community ties as a countervailing source of identity, the organization looms larger as a critical reference point.

Migration is not always bad. It has enabled the spread of cultural possibilities, cuisines, technologies, and strategies for civilization around the globe. It has provided new opportunities for immigrants and minority groups, and they, in turn, have introduced more cosmopolitan and global perspectives into the lives of ordinary people. More important, it has sometimes also aided the spread of the Christian theological views mentioned above.

Yet for organizational managers, moving has also typically pushed them away from family, church, and the local community as sources of personal identity; and they are simultaneously pulled toward the professional specialties and organizations within which they work. A significant investment has been required to obtain and maintain these managerial positions. They are launching pads for extended influence. Managerial theory endorses this investment of effort as the route to self-actualization and satisfaction. Geographic relocation compounds the problem. The result is that many managers are further encouraged to find their primary sense of identity in their paid professional work.

When the ingredient of sexual identity is thrown into this mix, the results can be highly volatile. If one's sex is seen as the ultimate source of one's identity, and one's identity rests primarily in self-actualization in the workplace, then any slight, perceived or real, of one's gendered sense of self is highly offensive. In addition, if the primary identity of either partner in the dual-career family is jeopardized by the successful relocation of only one member, both parties and perhaps the family commitments suffer. Blending a sexual foundation for personal identity with a vocational identity totally focused on one's organizational work is the basis for fireworks.

Vocation: A Christian View of Our Work

The belief that identity should arise primarily either from our biology or from our professional position is a major naturalist and secularist pitfall into which contemporary humans jump all too willingly. Both beliefs presume that life and work are exclusively centered in *human* existence and development. Looking for identity in either location ignores the role of God and the deeper, broader, more enduring realm of human responsibility. Christian ideas are an indispensable corrective of these views. The Christian framework for vocation offers an alternative to the exclusive connection of personal identity to biology and/or paid employment, both of which tempt managerial men and women.

Christian ideas about calling have gradually evolved since the time of Jesus. The early church accepted tentmakers like Paul and cloth dealers like Lydia. They could not afford to separate their work for the resurrected Christ from livelihoods and social contexts that provided for necessities. Yet within a few centuries the idea of Christian calling was interwoven with Greek structures of thought and society that valued contemplation as the highest good. Within that Grecian framework the monastic orders developed their interpretations of calling. The result, for Christians in the Middle Ages, was a strong emphasis on the contemplative life within the monastery as the path to God, a life unfettered by common social and economic interactions. While there were variations among the monastic orders, on the whole, thinking, worship, and prayer occupied the bulk of their time. Thus, in the Middle Ages most people saw Christian calling, principally, as separation from the ordinary work of society.[12]

However, by the time of the Reformation, emerging Protestants were discussing the concept of vocation at some length, questioning the separated framework for Christian calling that had been in place for almost a thousand years. Martin Luther believed a Christian sense of vocation combined our relationship with God, located in the kingdom of heaven, with service to God by loving our neighbors, located in the kingdom of earth. In *The Fabric of This World*, Lee Hardy describes Luther's concept of that service in the world:

> More precisely, a vocation is the specific call to love one's neighbor which comes to us through the duties which attach to our social

place or "station" within the earthly kingdom. A station in this life need not be a matter of paid employment, although it may be. As conceived by Luther, our stations include all the typical ways in which we are related to other people. Being a husband or a wife is a station in life, as well as being a parent or a child, a magistrate or a subject, a master or a servant, as well as a baker, a cobbler, or a farmer.[13]

In Luther's formulation, identity is tied to Christian vocation; and Christian vocation is tied to a whole host of stations, some of which are paid, but many of which are unrelated to paid employment. Instead, the many social roles that Christians fill, taken together, constitute their vocations. Thus, identity is found through the work one does to serve one's neighbors in a variety of social circumstances. It may involve a paid job but is not tied only to a paid job. While paid employment can have religious significance, it is not the only route through which humans participate in God's providence for the human race. It is only one part of vocation.

John Calvin agreed with Luther about the wide range of roles through which people should find their sense of Christian vocation; but Calvin placed more emphasis on serving God through active engagement in practical work. Specialization in employment was good because it allowed each person to use their unique talents. However, Calvin argued that the goal of that employment was not self-actualization but the building up of an interdependent human community which could serve one another.

Calvin, adopting a less static view of society, added one more critical caveat about paid employment. In his view, occupational structures are malleable. An occupation, as typically practiced, may not fit well with scriptural principles; particular occupations and the structure of occupations in a society can be corrupted by sin. In addition, new occupations can be created as innovative ways of organizing common life when society changes. As Lee Hardy summarizes Calvin's thought:

> therefore we are obliged to find a station in life where our gifts can indeed be employed for the sake of our neighbor's good. The station is no longer itself normative, but must be judged by its suitability as an instrument of social service. If it is found to be faulty or ill-adapted to its end, it must be either altered or discarded altogether. We must not only serve God in our calling; our calling itself must be brought into alignment with God's Word.[14]

Calvin's goal was not only that Christian vocation be seen as broad service in building the human community, but also that the human community recognize talents sometimes at odds with existing patterns of occupations. From Calvin's viewpoint it is our responsibility to not only participate in paid employment, but also to change the structures of paid employment to conform more closely with God's will.

While these Christian ideas about vocation are rooted in the Protestant Reformation, Catholic teachings increasingly have agreed with and sometimes expanded their sentiments. In *Centesimus Annus* Pope John Paul II argues for a broad understanding of vocation, encompassing both paid and unpaid roles, as well as for a restructuring of occupations to honor the contributions of all workers in organizational communities.[15]

Such Christian ideas about vocation have multiple implications for both personal choices and organizational/societal policy. On a personal level, they allow us to avoid many of the traps that develop when we, as managerial men and women, intertwine our personal and professional identities too tightly. They can help us as we search for career-related positions, as we plan for our own career development, and as we handle the disappointment and confusion we experience when our plans do not materialize.

When we, influenced by this more durable theology, incorporate both paid and unpaid work into our sense of vocation and acknowledge that occupations are also tainted by the Fall, as both females and males, we must consider the focus and balance of our work carefully. The goal of private corporate organizations is the provision of goods and services. Both men and women must ask which products and services best align with their creation responsibilities and care for their neighbors. Not all corporate products fit well in God's economy, but many can do so. We must find them and serve there.

However, as we plan for our career development we should do so in light of other obligations. We must also recognize limits to the effectiveness of our paid occupations in meeting the host of obligations we should shoulder. Paid managerial work must be balanced with the other vocational responsibilities that accrue during a particular period of adult life. These responsibilities will vary from person to person. They will depend, not only on one's sex, but also on the range and nature of one's family obligations, needs of one's church, obligations to one's community and nation, and a host of other considerations. The confluence of factors defining each person's realm of responsibilities will be unique.

It is important that we leave space and time for that broader realm of responsibilities, the realm beyond paid employment. That realm is much broader than the "mommy track" of career development attributed to Felice Schwartz, the founder of Catalyst, in the latter 1980s;[16] and it is much broader than the "parent track" for career development espoused by those scrambling to amend Schwartz's faux pax. That broader realm of responsibility is everything which belongs to vocation but is beyond the scope of paid employment. Along with paid professional work, men and women who build on this sound theological framework for their lives will sift through responsibilities to parents and children, spouse and church, local and global communities to discern the critical needs to which they have the talents to contribute.

Vocation is the use of our gifts as a response to God, listening closely to what the Lord requires from each of us. Vocation will be unique to each person. Multiple combinations of stations may answer God's call and in different sequences, rhythms, and balances. Each Christian's vocation will by definition be highly particular, fitted to unique gifts, opportunities, circumstances, and covenants to which we are already obliged. The result is that we must carefully discern which roles we should occupy, in what balance we should occupy them, and at what pace we should allow each of them to develop.

When one views vocation in this manner, finding the right path becomes a great daily adventure. Each day is filled with challenge but also with risk. It is quite possible that such a Christian view will not fit the current societal mold for managerial professionals. Such a perspective encourages a much broader vision of appropriate work. In some seasons of life, both males and females will need to leave or restructure their paid work to find a better balance in their vocations. Yet in other seasons of life some can devote more energy to paid work because other vocational obligations have been fulfilled. Possibilities for modification abound because those adopting such a Christian approach are solidly anchored in this sea of change.

However, one additional factor, already implicit, must be explicitly addressed. This theological viewpoint denies that we undertake the vocational adventure alone. Our vocations are also dependent on feedback from the rest of the human community. Vocation is not simply an independent quest. In a dynamic occupational environment, which John Calvin had just begun to experience in the 1500s, human motives are complex. We have aspirations based on imperfect information and limited insights. As a result we must rely on others to help us define our vocation. If one desires a particular position but an offer is not forthcoming, the judgment of others that this is not the best vocational match must be taken seriously. For it is in community that our choices about vocation are affirmed or denied. When the human community does not choose a person for a particular role, be it paid or unpaid, then one is not called to that role as part of one's vocation at that particular time. The judgment of the community is communicating otherwise.

The Christian concept of vocation is helpful during times when our paid employment takes a sharp and unexpected turn, perhaps when our careers seem lost, radically changed, or destroyed. In an era of globalization and corporate re-engineering there is no job security for those in the managerial profession. The requirements of corporations can change swiftly, sometimes savagely. Companies are more rapidly bought and sold. Organizations merge and break apart. New stakeholders bring different ideas about performance to boards of directors. In the process, senior executive positions to which we aspire can be eliminated or re-created with new responsibilities. We may then lack appropriate skills and qualities for such positions, causing great disappointment to those of us who aspire to such roles.

In such a fluid environment it is a major comfort to understand a full-orbed sense of Christian vocation. Though we'd rather remain blind to the facts, we can acknowledge that sometimes our quest for a particular position overreaches the appropriate boundaries on our vocation at a given time in our lives. Our knowledge and skills may not match the defined needs; or, even when we have the knowledge and skills, the range of our other unpaid vocational responsibilities may prevent us from being highly effective in particular roles. A strong understanding of Christian vocation can help us through our disappointment.

First-level and middle managers who feel the sting of change can also be helped by a Christian understanding of calling. When "right-sizing" forces role changes or even the disappearance of jobs, managers may be dismissed from the corporate culture to fend for themselves in defining future employment. Yet while losing our jobs because of organizational re-engineering is highly stressful, a Christian approach will not allow us to decide that we have lost our entire vocation in the process. We retain the portions of vocation that are not tied to paid employment and can find additional time to explore them, while working and waiting to restore the vocational piece that is paid employment.

What do these concepts imply when gender is added to the equation? In theological terms, not much. A full sense of Christian vocation applies equally to men and women. Both females and males must seek circumstances in which their gifts and creation responsibilities are a match with the organizational choices available; both must ponder carefully about the appropriate type and pace of career development; both must think about the balance of paid and unpaid aspects of vocation; both must involve the broader human community in the exploration and confirmation of their work-related gifts.

Yet a Christian concept of vocation, as describe above, prevents us from equating sexual biology with identity, or paid employment with vocation, the two mistakes we so frequently make in our culture. We are freed from existing cultural structures to discern the paths to which God calls each of us.

To summarize, we can be more effective in our service to God and our contributions to the kingdom when we avoid the two mistakes described above. Gender should be part of, but not the strongest root of, our Christian identity; and Christian identity found in vocation includes, but is much broader than, our paid employment. Thus, paid work in organizational life should not be primarily gender-based; but neither should life in these organizations overwhelm all other responsibilities for either men or women. We are free to develop our callings in innumerable ways. With this perspective, gender should be a *minor*, not a major, consideration in organizational life.

Yet both the structures of organizations and societies in which they operate are seriously damaged by sin. So in the next section we will look at the roles and responsibilities of leaders who manage an organizational climate in which gender has become a *major*, not a minor, matter.

Leadership: Human-to-Human Relationships

Christian leadership concentrates on *human-to-human* relationships within the framework of God's greater cosmos. Leadership focuses on humanity's desire to advance together in a shared sense of mission or purpose. In the previous section I described Christian vocations as the human response to God's call. Calling concerns the *God to human* relationship, given the talents, interests, and abilities with which human beings are endowed. However, Christian leaders focus on enabling appropriate responses to God as individuals of different gifts, capacities, and resources join their senses of calling to the broader purposes of an organizational group. These are the human-to-human relationships which form the nexus of leaders' work.

Now and into the next century organizational groups, both profit and not-for-profit, will be critical means through which God's creation and the coming kingdom are explored and developed. We should strive to understand the work of men and women who create these human organizational frameworks. In that context it is critical to understand the relationship of leaders and followers as they engage in the mutual quest to find their place between the extremes of individualism and collectivism.

On one end of the societal continuum, writers such as Robert Bellah describe the rampant individualism of contemporary North America, documenting a deteriorating sense of community belonging and obligation.[17] On the other end of the continuum, writers such as Pope John Paul II, in *Centesimus Annus*, decry the tight control of state socialism which squelched the development of individual initiative and creativity during its ideological reign.[18]

However, for most people in industrialized countries, a day-by-day sense of *personal* location and meaning is not defined by these extremes. They are not always torn by massive forces pulling them toward extreme individualism or debilitating state control. The sharp extremes of individualism and collectivism are ameliorated by the organizational communities in which people hold membership. These mediating structures balance needs for individuality with larger frames for daily meaning and common purpose. Thus, organizations serve important public as well as private functions. While they aid us because of the specific products and services they provide, they have a special ability and call to balance us between harsh loneliness and losing our lives in the herd.

One of the most important tasks of organizational leaders is to create the ties that bind human hearts together as they focus on organizational purposes, structures, and resources. Even when leaders must emphasize the strategic stewardship of financial, technological, and physical resources, they still materially affect the framework for meaning and direction of all who participate in, or are served by, the organization. Thus, the call to leadership in the world of organizations is a very significant one for men and women. It invites those who can lead to create the possibility that the goals, gifts, and aspirations of individual people can be blended into organizational missions that serve our human neighbors in numerous ways.

Yet the basis for effective leadership is not obvious. It is complex and even sometimes mysterious. Although leadership theorists have formally studied the leadership phenomena for well over seventy-five years, they are still frequently amazed at the path that leadership takes. Furthermore, in the past two decades the struggle to clarify the foundations for effective leadership has been greatly complicated by the overlay of gender. Some will argue that gender is a factor that not only does, but should, determine our leadership theories and styles. They believe that gender can and should be the basis for developing distinctly masculine and feminine styles of leadership.

What we think about the origins and models for leadership is important to the future of our organizational world. Yet I will argue against a gender-based theory of leadership and instead propose that more appropriate leadership foundations lie in well-grounded, faith-based concepts for human relationships. This foundation places gender theory in a much different context but it does not ignore the contribution of sex-based differences to the match between leaders and followers.

A thorough examination of Christian beliefs about leadership has been hampered by a certain amount of preconscious cultural conditioning rooted in social location. This has led to highly selective uses of scriptural authority in conjunction with prevailing managerial theory. That positioning has led some to take comfort in a top-down theory of leadership and others to celebrate a bottom-up approach, both of which can be found in the Scripture and in tradition.

Historically, some readily embraced a strongly top-down theory of leadership. Its emphasis on good order and proper respect for those placed in authority resonated with the words of Hebrews 13:17, "Obey your leaders and submit to their authority" (NIV). This emphasis and style fit well with, and may have facilitated, some of the developments that made possible not only the West in general, but the United States in particular. Certainly this model harmonized with the predominantly white male Protestant establishment and the classical managerial theory espoused at the beginning of the twentieth century. Like their Catholic and Jewish predecessors in Europe, North American women, immigrants, and unskilled laborers had more limited educations and few legal rights. Even if the predominant authoritarian style should have been questioned in light of the whole message of the Gospel, circumstances made the old, traditional patterns reasonably workable. Caucasian males' access to more extensive education and professional role models did prepare them to be the business, political, and religious leaders of the time. Logically, organizational directions, decisions, and communications were controlled by this small privileged group.

These traditional patterns were reinforced by the theories of Max Weber, Henry Fayol, and Frederick Taylor in the late 1800s and early 1900s. While each developed specific ideas about managing organizations, all of their theories emphasized that work was more efficiently done if it was subdivided into small discrete units of activity with clear boundaries and a clear hierarchy of authority.[19]

Yet, practically, the top-down model of leadership became more and more unworkable over time. A democratic, pluralistic society was attractive to people from a broad range of backgrounds, and some turned to an inverted, bottom-up model, sometimes even in revolutionary or counter-cultural terms. In a society with changing demographics, higher levels of education, and paid employment that was gradually more knowledge-based, leaders realized that they were no longer managing the meek, mild sheep of earlier decades. Effectively motivating and managing skilled employees with special areas of expertise required a different leadership model.

Furthermore, many of those who embraced faith-based Christian principles had simultaneously grown much more skittish about the authoritarian mantle of power. In part this occurred because of a new wave of managerial theory—the behavioral school first espoused by Elton Mayo in the 1930s[20] and carried forward by Douglas McGregor's 1960 book, *Theory X/Theory Y*.[21] These behavioral theorists placed a much stronger emphasis on understanding and cultivating human relations in the workplace. That questioning of authoritarian approaches to leadership also occurred in part because many rediscovered that Jesus' emphasis on humility was not completely dismissed from the Western heritage. Focused consideration of Jesus' injunctions that "the last shall be first" (Matt. 19:30, NIV) and "he who is least among you all—he is the greatest" (Luke 9:48, NIV) fit the cultural mood of the 1960s and 1970s. Christians, after all, are warned against personal ambition, self aggrandizement, and the quest for personal power. Acknowledging this has led many, some centuries ago but others in the past few decades, to reject authoritarian forms of leadership as incompatible with the biblical message. This rejection also fit with the characteristics of a changing labor force.

Many who were looking for faith-based principles began instead to embrace the leadership model identified as "servant leadership." The contemporary title given to this model originated from Robert Greenleaf's well-read 1977 book *Servant Leadership*.[22] Greenleaf, writing out of a Quaker tradition, actually focused much of his book's analysis on the exercise of leadership by individuals who serve on organizational boards of directors. He decried the passive caretaker model, which he believed characterized organizational trustees of that decade. Greenleaf offered "servant leadership," a public sense of active dutiful servanthood, as an alternate model for public trustees. Over time, though, the meaning that Greenleaf had assigned to "servant leadership" was altered. It became associated with internal organizational leadership, not external trusteeship, which had been Greenleaf's original concern.

Using the servant-leadership motif, some Christian thinking about leadership has turned organizational charts upside down in the past few decades. The example of servant leadership typically invoked by Christians is that of Jesus washing the feet of his disciples. By implication organizational leaders should humbly seek to meet the sometimes simple needs of employees. Sometimes organizational charts have been redrawn with the CEO positioned at the bottom, instead of the top of the chart, as someone who serves the whole and supports the flourishing of others. More authority for organizational decisions is given to middle managers and even entry-level employees. Overall, it is presumed that people will perform more effectively if leaders give them authority and responsibility.

There is some inherent good in the servant-leadership approach to organizational decision making. It opens organizations to responsibility and participation by a broader array of personnel. This model more adequately recognizes the special gifts each employee brings to the work environment and allows greater opportunity for the growth of those talents. Servant leadership properly emphasizes that good organizational leaders must be responsive to employees.

Yet, for all its positive features, there are significant dangers in this model for those who wish to lead in a Christian manner. Such a vision does not completely honor the example of Jesus. It can often result in poor organizational stewardship, and it may be dishonest about real decision processes.

A closer look at the example of Jesus is instructive. Though Jesus gave his life for his followers, he did not simply succumb to their sense of his mission or their design of his path. Instead he brought his own sense of vocation, his profound knowledge of the tradition, and mental readiness for dealing with people from many groups and classes to his work with the disciples. Jesus was not simply an empty vessel, though he emptied himself for humanity. Thus, to perceive leadership primarily as a conduit for the desires of followers is not true to the life that Jesus lived.

Second, use of this model may result in poor organizational stewardship. Leaders who abdicate a direct role in presenting ideas for the organization's future presume that the only appropriate model for the flow of ideas and decision making is a bottom-up, consensus-building one; and bottom-up consensus may not be effective in honing organizational futures in a new century. Consensus decisions may result in ambiguous, watered-down strategies and policies required to keep *everyone* invested in a process. The process itself may need to be repeatedly refined and revised, using up a significant amount of workplace time. The result may be an organization wandering from its central mission, fragmented in its strategy, wedded to outmoded paradigms, or buried under the sheer weight of the decision process.

In a time when resources were abundant and the needs of organizational stakeholders were less complex, the problems of organizational wandering, fragmentation, datedness, and slower movement were not as critical. The desire to experiment could be easily financed. When human energy was focused on the wrong priorities, there was sufficient capacity to absorb such excess and bounce back. However, economic globalization and technological change have significantly altered the environment within which both profit and not-for-profit organizations operate.

Globalization and costly technological investments continue to press industrialized nations to utilize human labor more efficiently as worldwide product, price, and wage competition become more critical. Together these factors create much greater complexity in decisions about employees, customers, products, and markets. They accelerate change and shift needs for human, financial, and physical resources. The result is a much smaller margin for organizational error than was true in the 1960s.

In such a turbulent environment with less slack, vision must be focused. Strategies must be tightly defined. Priorities must be clear. Efficiencies must be high. There can be little tolerance for the organizational wandering which may be encouraged by a servant-leadership approach. To allow such may endanger the organization's very survival and its ability to serve customers and sustain the lives of its employees. Such poor stewardship violates the trust that our Creator places in leaders.

Third, we can ask whether the servant-leadership model is really honest about what usually transpires in the decision-making process. Why would those who have leadership knowledge, skills, and vision become only empty vessels waiting to be filled by followers? If leaders are truly qualified, they bring years of relevant education and experience to their work. To build a leadership model which presumes that they will not use their developed expertise is either wasteful of their talents or blind to reality. Honesty requires us to expect deep personal contributions from organizational leaders.

Therefore, despite the seemingly comfortable fit between concepts of servant leadership and a superficial reading of Scriptures, the servant-leadership model may not be either the most biblical or the most effective one in serving organizations in the decades ahead.

Attributing Leadership to Gender

The search for an appropriate Christian leadership model is further compounded when differing styles of leadership are attributed to gender. When social scientists write about differences between men and women, popular culture presumes that these can be translated into gender-based leadership differences. The social science writings by scholars such as Joan Acker, Mary Belenky, Patricia Hill Collins, and Carol Gilligan[23] have focused on the ways in which women differ from men in modes of understanding, psychological development, career paths, and frameworks for ethical decision making. For many, it's a relatively simple leap to then presume gender-based leadership differences exist. From that assumption they then work to develop gender-based *theories* of leadership, a school of thought now emerging.

The popular perception about gender-based leadership theory is that a male style will be more directive and political while a female style will be more nurturing and supportive. Men are presumed to be command-oriented bosses and women are presumed to be responsive nurturers who meet people's needs. These presumptions lead to interesting consequences in some circles. Males in leadership have been attacked as presumed authoritarians and instructed to let their nurturing qualities emerge. Females in leadership are challenged to take "assertiveness training" and become more aggressive in their leadership.

The discussion becomes even more convoluted when differentiations are made between more masculine and feminine styles within each sex. The masculine and the feminine are tied to abstract concepts of gender not directly connected with biological sex differences. It then becomes possible to discuss both sexes as those who use a more masculine or a more feminine approach to leadership. A male can be encouraged to use either a masculine or feminine leadership style, as can a female; and in such theorizing after a certain point it is exceptionally difficult to know what tiger one has by what tail.

For all men and women this greatly complicates the adoption of an effective Christian leadership style. A male manager may see the cultivation of close relationships with subordinates as too feminine, or he may choose a hard-driving, power-conscious approach as appropriately masculine. A female manager might wonder whether her press to become more strategically focused is seen as too masculine; or she may eschew care for subordinates because she believes a masculine model of leadership to be more acceptable in her operational culture.

There are aspects of leadership that do differ because we are men and women. Our physiologies, our socialization, our career paths, and the barriers to participation have not been the same for males and females. Yet to acknowledge this does not require the presumption that sexual differences or related gender theorizing should be the foundation on which we develop our guiding theories of leadership. Doing so prevents individual men and women from adopting a blended leadership style which best suits their unique gifts and their specific organizational circumstances.

Leadership approaches should, to some degree, be contingent on the circumstances at hand. The task-driven company may need a leader who cheerleads. The warm responsive company may need a leader who clearly defines work challenges. A floundering company may need a strong directive hand. A growing company may need the breathing room of a bottom-up style. A freewheeling employee may need structure imposed. A damaged employee may need empathetic support.

We unnecessarily limit the flexibility of our responses to changing circumstances when we, first of all, label leadership styles as female and male or feminine and masculine. Every leader, whether female or male, should be encouraged to build a full range of leadership strategies and responses. While cognizant of female/male differences, we should base our leadership theories primarily on such analysis. The results are complicated, inhibiting, and not grounded in the faith-based foundations that should most matter to us.

So now, at the end of the century, leaders should consider both gender-based leadership theory and the assignment of top-down and bottom-up models of leadership specifically to males and females as simplistic. Are male/female, top/bottom the only categories by which we can think of human relations?

Besides, leaders must continue to lead. We live in an era where organizations without a strong sense of direction, without shapers of organizational perception, without senior interpreters of organizational reality, will flounder. Both female and male leaders must struggle to find a biblical vision for leadership that diligently avoids the pitfalls of gender-labeled leadership as well as the top-down/bottom-up dichotomy.

A larger vision must guide our reading of the contingencies of the situation. As we move toward the year 2000 we should ground our leadership theories and styles in our deepest values about human relationships. And, if we dig deeply, these will inevitably be religious. If leadership is first of all about the human-to-human connection, what is the scriptural basis for that relationship? And what will be the outcome of leadership with a biblical foundation?

A More Biblical Leadership Foundation

Without human relationships there is no reason to steward financial, physical, or technological resources, for there would be no customers, no stockholders, no suppliers, and no employees. There would be no one to serve with all of our organizational capacity. Thus, the foundation for leadership should be the norms and purposes for human relationships in a group setting that reach as high and wide, as deep and long, as we can discover. Christians believe that these have been, at least in part, identified in the Scriptures. Its message directs those with administrative gifts to use them in bringing together the gifts of others in service to God and the human community.

In the discussion about the variety of spiritual gifts which serve the Body of Christ in 1 Corinthians 12, Paul identifies administrative ability as a specific spiritual gift. The gift of administration, what leaders do, is mentioned specifically where Paul writes, "And in the church God has appointed first of all apostles, second prophets, third teachers, then workers of miracles, also those having gifts of healing, those able to help others, *those with gifts of administration* (emphasis mine), and those speaking in different kinds of tongues" (v. 28, NIV).

However, while leadership is a differentiable gift, it does not follow that what flows from it is in anyway greater or lesser than any other gift. This passage portrays human relationships as relationships among equals, all of whom have differing gifts and tasks. Paul does not agree that one gift is better than any other or one person better than any other. Earlier in the same chapter Paul writes that "There are different kinds of gifts, but the same Spirit" (v. 4, NIV) and "All these [i.e., gifts] are the work of the one and the same Spirit, and he gives them to each one, just as he determines." (v. 11, NIV). The consistent biblical message in the New Testament is one in which God sees human gifts as equally honorable regardless of their varied distribution.

Finally, the purpose for the administrative gift in conjunction with all other gifts is building up the human community in service to God and each other. Paul is specifically addressing the church with his organic metaphor of the hand, foot, ear, and eye as necessary parts of a well-functioning body. However, the biblically organized church illustrates some of the Christian values that also should be embedded in corporate forms of organization. Those groups should also be framed by the understanding that coordination of individual gifts for the well-being of the community is a primary means for serving God.

So, in the context of equal human relationships, the gift of administration is recognized as a specific gift within the human society. Leadership is only one gift among other equally respected gifts; but it is a gift which operates to connect the myriad of other talents which together contribute to the well-being of human communities. If this perspective is a decisive biblical basis for understanding leadership, we can then ask if there are any contemporary theories of leadership that correspond well with this viewpoint.

The transformational school of leadership thinking reflects this theory quite well. Though its ideas are not couched in religious terms and may not first have developed from faith-based considerations, transformational leadership theory is more compatible with Christian thinking about leadership than are many other models. It is more viable for the organizational environment of the 1990s and beyond.

The modern transformational school of leadership grew from the work of James McGregor Burns, Bernard Bass, Joseph Badaracco, Richard Ellsworth, and others between the late 1970s and the early 1990s.[24] These theorists worked to create a model which abandoned both top-down and bottom-up approaches to leadership. Instead, they observed the behavior of truly successful leaders and their followers in a variety of settings, both white and blue collar. They developed an approach to leadership which dug deeper into the complexities of the leader/follower relationship and the push and pull that exists within it.

The transformational model of leadership for both men and women emphasizes equal honor in the leader/follower relationships. For example, in this model an organizational chart that identifies the lines of responsibility is not held perpendicular to the desktop, with the senior leadership identified at either the top or the bottom of the organization. Instead, the chart lies flat on the table. All members of the organization are seen as contributing their gifts, with leader/follower relations seen as sideways relationships among those of equal honor. Leaders can pop up from any position on that flat organizational chart to animate the ongoing organizational story. The model places little value in hierarchy. In this theory anyone, under a particular set of circumstances, may be called to lead. Those not previously identified as public organizational leaders can become such under the right circumstances. Like Poland's Lech Walesa or the NAACP's Myrlie Evers-Williams, someone may be called to lead when they do not expect it. Such leaders may arise from little-known sources, but they respond when needed. They may be night supervisors of a new plant or volunteers who respond with CPR in a crisis. These are the "water carriers" and "roving leaders" whom Max DePree, author and retired CEO of Herman Miller Corporation, describes in his essays about leadership.[25] These are the people who take leadership responsibility every day in any organization's quest to accomplish its mission.

No matter who takes responsibility for leadership, the transformational model vigorously promotes the idea of leadership as a two-way street, honoring both parties in the organizational covenant. Leaders develop the process for finding a common direction, but they expect followers to contribute their ideas for determining the future. The contributions of followers may alter the sense of direction that the organization develops. Likewise, leaders are allowed to bring their own visions, values, and plans to the organization. They take an active hand in shaping organizational direction and may alter followers' sense of the organizational future.

However, everything the leader brings—values, visions, abilities, or disabilities—can be scrutinized by those being led. The person leading is always in relationship to followers; and that relationship requires not only that the leader bring change to the organization but that the leader allow himself or herself to be changed by followers. The principal requirement of the leader is to structure two-way paths of influence to build goals, values, and directions for the organization—but that path of influence runs in both directions.

The scrutiny and honest feedback which are part of this model may bring challenge and pain, but it is also likely to bring new learning and positive change. The leader must hear what followers are saying and see what they are doing. The effective leader will learn from them just as they, in turn, learn from the one who is leading. This model of leadership leaves no one the same. All people involved in human leader/follower relationships are necessarily changed by the activity of leading and following. That is the nature of genuine human relationship.

This transformational model of leadership more accurately reflects the message of Scripture about human relationships. It honors the differentiation of gifts more clearly than does the servant-leadership model. Thus those who are gifted in "administration" should lead in those roles which channel individual interests and talents into service for the good of the whole organization. Those with an administrative gift should not be afraid to use it, as long as they view it as only one among the many necessary talents in the organization.

If one accepts this model of leadership as the closest contemporary equivalent to a Christian-leadership model, what are the implications for the leadership and gender question?

Transformational leadership is not a *gender-based* model. It is first and foremost a model based on certain assumptions about *human* relationships without adding characterizations of gender to the equation. However, the model, because of its focus on the interactive relationship between leaders and followers, still allows differences which might reasonably be attributed to sexuality to function in any person asked to lead. In this setting all leaders or followers, whether female or male, may and should bring themselves as whole persons to the leader/follower relationship. Leaders will make decisions as male and female beings with particular types of experiences, some of which have occurred because of their biological sex and others of which are connected to the cultural experiences of their sex. Making decisions as a whole person is encouraged in a transformational leadership model.

Yet a model for leadership that accepts sexually differentiated selves in the leadership relationship is far different from a theory that bases its leadership model primarily on gender. Instead of developing our leadership theories on the basis of gender, we should root them principally in faith and a scriptural understanding of human relationships. The transformational approach is far superior to any gender-based theory in this regard.

Matching Organizations and Leaders

Ideally, leadership should develop as a two-way match of gifts equally honored between leaders and followers; but finding and sustaining a good match between leaders and followers is a highly complex process. Like any other human undertaking operating within history's borders, the experience of the leader/follower relationship is permeated by both the promise of *shalom* and the persistent effects of sin. Both are present but the proportion is critical to the quality of this intimate human match.

In such a context it is exceptionally difficult to distinguish how much one's sex, in comparison with other factors, complicates the sense of a leadership match and the reactions to a nonmatch by leaders and organizations. While gender-based differences should not be the basis for our theories and models of leadership, sex-based roles in the broader society do affect the context for leadership choices, the developmental paths of emerging leaders, and organizational decisions about who should lead. We can consider each of these factors in light of ideas about gender.

Gender's Role in Matching Leaders and Organizations

Broad societal ideas about gender affect organizational contexts for choosing a leader. Society's framework shapes expected gender roles and meanings which, in turn, frame an organization's perceptions about whom they should consider for leadership.

For example, an organization may feel uncomfortable when considering a married woman with children at home for a leadership position. Even if she is well qualified for leadership, those on the selection committee may not be able to imagine ways in which she could arrange her life to be an effective parent and an effective public leader. Yet that doubt may never arise in their consideration of a male candidate. Why not? Because the broader society presumes that the *daily* responsibilities for managing a household and raising children reside more fully with women than with men. Women are the ones typically perceived to be in charge of organizing the cleaning, cooking, laundry, and social life, along with school schedules, homework, sports/arts events, and transportation. Because the broader societal context provides few models for alternative family arrangements, it may be much more difficult for those choosing a leader to place their confidence in a middle-aged married woman than a man of similar circumstances.

In some situations their doubts may be warranted. However, even if such a woman is the most qualified candidate and has a spouse eager to accommodate her leadership opportunity, the selection committee may be unable to overcome its doubts about her capacity to sustain the intense organizational focus required of a good leader. The social framework makes it too difficult for them to imagine a married female who now does not, or soon may not, have primary responsibility for managing a household and children. The selection committee may place such a high value on family as well as organizational life that they, in good conscience, agree to screen out this candidate in everyone's best interests.

However, in this example, an expectation about gendered societal roles prevents the organization from carefully considering all of its options. The societal context for the decision has colored the reality that the selection committee sees; and the committee may have failed to imagine new organizational possibilities which are within their reach in contemporary society. Still, society's more abstract symbolic understanding of gender also intersects with organizational choices. For example, the masculine is more typically associated with facile use of power than is the feminine. Suppose an organizational search committee is asked to compare Evan and Emily for a leadership position. Unless the committee takes significant time to delve into the work experience records of the two applicants, they may choose Evan because they presume that, being male, he has the ability to wield power effectively and make the "hard" decisions. Masculinity is then being associated with the necessary toughness to be a successful organizational leader. By comparison, committee members may be unconsciously worried that Emily's exercise of power will be too "soft" since "softness" is associated with femininity and organizational ineffectiveness. They may perceive that it is somehow "unnatural" for Emily to handle power and authority well.

Yet the opposite might also occur based on gender stereotypes. Emily may be chosen because she is perceived to bring that inherent female compassion to the job, a valuable trait when the organization is downsizing or when customer service is critical to survival. In these environments female empathy is seen as a nice counterbalance to male leaders perceived as hard-driving simply because they are male.

In either case, organizational decision making is not based primarily on the available evidence. Decisions are filtered through layers of what are accepted as appropriate gender roles and meanings in a society. These filters create dynamics in the organization's decisions about leaders; such decisions are based on perception, not concrete reality.

There may be no way around such perceptions for either men or women who aspire to leadership. No individual or organization functions without a perceptual lens. Perceptions help us shape and organize the world so that there is some relative stability of sense and meaning in our lives. We rely on our assumptions about the meaning of masculinity and femininity to function in society. However, when organizations link a society's framework for the masculine and feminine to its perceptions about those aspiring to leadership, problems are bound to occur.

In addition to analyzing the societal context, the individuals who aspire to leadership must also be considered when searching for a good leader/follower match. Effective leaders are always learning to manage their ambitions and their readiness to lead. Leaders should question the fit of their personal goals with the ambitions of an organization and the timeliness of a match between their contribution and organizational needs.

However, an appropriate sense of ambition to lead may develop differently in men and women. Through most of the twentieth century, women have been principally positioned to develop competence and ambition in the private, domestic sphere. Their ambitions have historically been tied to the needs and aspirations of their families. For many women twentieth-century history has provided relatively few female models who effectively managed their *public* ambitions related to broader organizations.

Women aspiring to leadership may have more struggles in accepting and managing their own sense of public ambition than do men. They may question whether it is appropriate to have public ambition when they have typically seen themselves as the servants of others. They may have more difficulties dealing with unmet aspirations since they have less experience in the rough and tumble of the career jungle.

The readiness to lead may also develop differently in men and women. Because of biology and socialization the developmental paths of men and women as adults are frequently dissimilar. Many women gravitate toward public leadership when they have first resolved the private issues of marriage and family. Some women who remain single gradually become more serious about their careers only when they presume that marriage and children are less likely options. Others turn to professional life as a primary focus after bearing children and meeting the constant needs of youngsters. We know that generally the patterns of paid participation in the labor force are not the same for married women as for men. Thus, many women finish their educations later than men, often as older adult students, and commitments to their nuclear or extended families may constrain their choices of institutions for advanced education and their geographic mobility related to job changes. The paths of education and employment that prepare women for leadership, and the ages at which they feel comfortable moving into public leadership, may be different than for men. While in a perfect world such differentiations in educational and employment backgrounds should not exist, they do in fact exist, given the dominant presumptions about appropriate gender roles in North American society. The paths of the specific individuals involved will differ, and one's sex will influence that difference.

Finally, the role of one's sex in choosing leaders is affected by both formal organizational polices and the informal organizational culture. Some organizations do not believe that female/male equity in the leadership ranks is a high priority. Thus, they take much less time to understand the differences in the life cycles of adult males and females. They are not prepared to understand the more in-and-out paths through paid employment or constrained choice sets for education, which may be more characteristic of females than males. Organizations may interpret these accommodations to life circumstances as weaknesses that somehow "damage" preparation for leadership. Such organizational perceptions can prevent selection committees from clearly seeing the leadership potential of an applicant.

Other organizations have determined that employment equity between the sexes is a high priority for them. Based on ethical convictions or sex discrimination laws and related court rulings, some decision makers sense a responsibility to enhance selection and development of both female and male leaders. Yet these organizations are torn between the goals of affirmative action and the struggle to implement it in ways that are equitable and fair for both sexes. They vacillate between a desire to promote more women into leadership arenas, thus breaking the "glass ceiling," and a commitment to sex-blind analysis based on the track record of accomplishments and organizational loyalty.

The organizational climate for selecting leaders is further complicated when these concerns about sexual equality are considered in conjunction with changes in the competitive environment or the culture of an organization. The risk-averse leader may lose the edge when new technology turns a stable industry on its head. The risk-embracing leader may lose the confidence of followers when they need a period of consolidation and stability. Attempts of leaders, either male or female, to shift their dominant strategy and style may fall short and little can be done to bridge the widening gap. The resulting decisions to change those holding formal leadership positions may lead to charges of sex discrimination, even when decisions to change the leadership team were made on other grounds.

Is it at all surprising in this environment that finding an effective match between leaders and organizations is a difficult task, fraught with the possibility of error and gender-based bias in one direction or another? In a sinful world effective matches between organizational requirements for leadership and those aspiring to leadership are not easy to create. Societal gender stereotypes cloud perceptions of reality; those aspiring to lead handle personal ambition and readiness differently; organizations struggle to balance sex-based equity with fairness to all.

Our human limitations will always thwart perfect matches. Leaders may perceive that they are right and good matches at a particular time in the life of the organization, even when organizations do not see it that way. An organization may pursue a particular leader who is not convinced of the call to lead this group of people at this particular time. Both leaders and organizations can mistakenly put aside underlying misgivings about a match, which often resurface later in painful ways. Female/male considerations greatly complicate the whole undertaking.

Sometimes, just sometimes, the marriage of a leader and organization works. The goals, the readiness, the perceptions, the timeliness, and the context come together. Yet, given organizational change and environmental turbulence, sustaining a successful match over time may be just as difficult as the creation of the original match.

All leaders, both female and male, and their organizations must come to grips with the strong possibility of failure and the fragility of success in creating matches between aspiring leaders and organizations. We must acknowledge that, try as we might to avoid these pitfalls, including those which inappropriately associate our sexual differences with leadership, we see through a glass darkly. The only path through this murky future is the path of faith in a God who creates good in both leadership failure and leadership success.

The Challenge of Failure

Failure and disappointment create reactions of hostility, self-doubt, depression, or even organizational sabotage in aspiring leaders. Because aspiring leaders place tremendous weight on their paid public roles as a centerpiece of their lives, failure crushes the life in them, sometimes temporarily and sometimes permanently. A lack of success damages self-definition and a sense of public direction.

All female and male leaders react to failure. It is hard to say whether managing failure is more difficult for men or women leaders. Men may feel the weight of great expectations that they have not met. Women may struggle because of less experience in job-related failure and less developed coping skills—or the opposite may be true. Women may feel that they did not meet great self-expectations or the hopes of the communities which supported their quest. Men may be challenged by their first experience of leadership failure. There may be nothing inherently sex-based in their reactions to failure; those reactions may depend less on sex and more on the confluence of many individual factors.

However, all aspiring leaders must develop means for absorbing and coping with failure, both those within and beyond their control. Leaders must have a place to go with their thoughts and emotions. Here too, we should turn to theological reflection, specifically to the idea of a Trinitarian God.

God the Creator is sovereign over the purposes and end results of human history. God will continue to work out these created purposes in the lives of both individuals and organizations. The failure to achieve or maintain a match between a leader and an organization need not result in evil since God always works for the good of those who love God and are called according to God's purposes. An aspiring leader will not always understand the intersection of human sin, human limitations, and the will of God, but can live with the assurance that God watches over "your going out and your coming in from this time on and fovevermore" (Ps. 121:8). The Creator God is always at work weaving the threads of history into a more complete tapestry.

To be sure, sometimes that finished, perfect composition is too far beyond time's horizon. We can only barely glimpse its outline. Only distortions, frayed fibers, and frustrations seem to reign. At such times, believers turn to Jesus Christ as a model for coping with failure. Jesus' life and death invite a compassion for those who suffer because of professional failure or disappointment. His was a misunderstood vocation and he was rejected by followers who professed to love him most. While the career disappointments of aspiring leaders are inconsequential compared to the sacrifice of Christ, leaders can still know that their Redeemer suffers for them and with them. Both females and males can know a fellowship in suffering that goes even beyond the balm that family or friends may provide.

With this in mind, we can also believe that the Holy Spirit continues to build the fruits of love, joy, peace, patience, kindness, goodness, faithfulness, gentleness, and self-control. The Spirit will continue to build lives privately even when public lives are a shambles. Neither leaders nor followers can control public circumstances, even when it is the vocation of some to order segments of public life. But all can work to reinvent their private attitudes and responses as they let the Spirit work in them. From failure and disappointment can grow grace, goodness, compassion, understanding, and new direction for all aspiring to lead, female and male, if we allow God to work. There is nothing gendered about the Christian belief that we must allow the whole of the Trinity to invade our lives at the points of our career disappointments. Both men and women must learn to trust the purposes of their Creator and allow Jesus to carry them in their hurt. Both men and women can learn to let the Holy Spirit create new life in them, including forgiveness of any organizational decisions mistakenly based on gender.

Saying this does not diminish the struggles with personal feelings and organizational loyalties that occur when an effective match between a leader and organization is not made or sustained. Both those who aspire to lead and the organizations searching for a match will go through deep valleys in the process. Aspiring leaders not chosen will struggle to find another place to be effective. Rejected organizations will reassess their purposes, their values, and their attractiveness.

Yet, for us, both male and female, there is Someone more deeply at work in the world than it is possible for us to fathom. When aspiring leaders and followers do not properly find each other, kingdom progress does not stop. It simply takes other paths in our lives and the lives of organizations.

The Challenge of Success

Yet, on occasion, effective matches between leaders and followers do occur. Organizational selection committees are determined to find the right match regardless of sexual differences. They are focused on ability and the track record of real experience. They thoroughly do their homework about applicants. They accurately assess the organization's goals and needs. The person asked to fill the position is similarly convinced that he or she is able, ready, and well matched to the organization. The initial match is successful.

However, an initially successful match is no guarantee for the future. The external environment of an organization may change, legally, economically, or culturally. The nature of competition and cooperation faced by an organization may be turned on its head by emerging technologies and new global sources of competition. Internally, previously subordinated groups may mature and their preferred approach to products, people, resources, and problems may differ.

If one accepts the transformation theory of leadership as a good model for dynamic Christian leadership, then even an initially effective leader/follower match can only be sustained through continuing conversation, deep and sustained learning, and strong covenants of commitment to common goals. No leader ever stays the same; no follower ever stays the same; and no situation is static.

Deep and sustained learning must occur on several levels and in several ways. It can require intense digging into an organization's sense of its mission; intense listening to customers; or intense concern for individual employees. Such learning may involve the use of consultants, market research results, or the employee grapevine. Yet learning between leaders and followers is critical to continuing an effective leadership match.

To continue to be successful, one of the areas in which all leaders must keep learning is their understanding of sex and gender. When societal expectations about gender have changed substantially, and when the vast majority of new employees in the next twenty-five years will come from a pool of women, minorities, and immigrants, leaders must learn more about the influence of sex-based differences in the workplace. It is a necessary part of their continuous learning about the composition of the workforce which they lead. They must know more about the differences in adult life cycle between men and women. They must recognize the historical struggle of women desiring equal pay for equal work. They must hear the frustrations of men whose careers have hit a long plateau. They must understand the desire of women to break the glass ceiling into senior management. They must sense the frustration of men bypassed because they are men. Learning about the dynamics of sex-based identity is important for all leaders if they wish to translate their learning into effective plans for the organization's future.

An initial match between leaders and followers does not guarantee future success. Keeping the long-run covenant of leadership and followership alive is not easy. Especially when leadership is seen as a two-way partnership between leaders and followers, there are no straight paths to senior leadership and no guaranteed destinations for either men or women. For those aspiring to senior leadership and for the organizations they lead there are few, if any, organizational rules which hold under all circumstances. Mysteries about the influence of sex on leadership style and the choosing of leaders will never be perfectly clear. There are no guarantees about the road map, the quality of the road, the potential of detours, or rewards upon arrival. In fact there is no arrival. The organizational road continues beyond the horizon of human understanding.

Understanding the nature of this long and winding road puts organizational theory and leadership itself in perspective. Ultimately we have but one leader, and that person is not any of us. Nothing we can do by ourselves, organizationally, will finally usher in the New Jerusalem. We must depend on God for we cannot control or construct ultimate destiny.

Thus, effective leaders, female or male, never really arrive. They simply continue to develop, as they polish their skills and do God's bidding faithfully each day. If leaders embrace a Christian approach, they only work to become more the people whom God intended them to be in relationship to all those with whom they are associated. There is little more to which truly good leaders, men and women alike, need aspire.

Culture: Creating the Organizational Ethos

Shaping organizational culture is the third facet of our work. Vocation, the first facet, is our continuing quest to cultivate the divine/human relationship in work activities. Leadership, the second facet, involves human-to-human relationships as individual leaders and followers seek mutual purposes that join their efforts together. Organizational culture, the third facet, focuses on the relationship of managerial leaders to the organizational ethos which they cultivate.

An organization's culture consists of the values, beliefs, understandings, and norms shared by its members. It is shaped by two sets of factors. Informal factors, those typically described in textbook definitions of the organizational script, include the stories, symbols, heroes, slogans, and ceremonies of the organization.[26] However, the culture of an organization is also fundamentally shaped by the formal factors, the job descriptions, policy handbooks, and evaluation/reward structures put in place. Together, these informal and formal influences operate to make the organization's sense of communal purpose and story a colorful description of life together.

Managerial leaders are not the only ones who cultivate an organization's ethos. Its flavor is certainly the blend of all those who touch the organization, adding to the mix. Yet effective leaders, based on learning and experience, are among those most knowledgable of the recipe for an enjoyable and effective organizational culture. They often know what ingredients are lacking or when they have been mixed in the wrong proportions. Senior managers typically are also those who make the decisions about timing, how long an organizational mix must set for the yeast to work or how intensely it should bake without burning the results. Thus, while many cooks add to the finished feast, leaders are the head chefs of organizational culture.

Cultivating and cooking the organizational ethos is the arena in which managerial leaders make one of their primary contributions to the shape of human history. The life of any organization is relatively small when compared to the universal cosmos or even the stage for world events. Although some multinational corporations are larger than some nation-states, organizations are not typically the public setting in which nations interact with other nations; they rarely provide material for written political history. Yet every organization develops understandings about the principles and standards that guide the work and interaction of people who are connected to it. What an organization's people value together will shape their sense of priority, process, and policy. These, in turn, significantly influence the quality of the products and services rendered, the nature of life experienced inside the organization, and the values and ideas which spill into life outside the organization. The organizational ethos that managerial leaders cultivate is an important part of the social history that we write as groups of people in modern society. Thus, the organizational cultures that we shape are critical to the future.

Enabling healthy life in organizations is no easy undertaking. These cultures are less stable than in previous decades. Organizational boundaries have become more permeable with multiple rounds of growth, downsizing, resurgence, mergers, takeovers, and disaggregations. Some theorists now describe organizations as "shamrocks" in which each leaf represents a set of people with different relationships to the enterprise. On the first leaf reside smaller numbers of core employees; on the second, contractual groups to whom work is outsourced regularly; and on the third, a flexible labor force of part-time and temporary workers. Together these leaves make the organizational shamrock more fluid and changeable since each leaf has a different set of commitments to, arrangements with, and expectations of the organization.[27]

In this more turbulent environment gender-related issues are one aspect of organizational culture on which leaders must lead. Given decades of gender turmoil, it is imperative that leaders consciously take responsibility for the influence of gender on the organizational culture. In the tinderbox of organizational life, gender concerns are ignored to our peril.

For practical reasons leaders should be in the forefront of actions which create a healthier intersection between gender concerns and the broader organizational culture. The composition of the labor force continues to shift. In both North America and around the globe, women entering the paid labor force will constitute a significant source of new labor force participants for the next several decades. That shift in composition alone creates many factors which press for change.

Furthermore, that changing composition occurs against the historical backdrop of inequality in the United States. Only a little over one hundred years ago women could not legally own or inherit property, a principle means of income and wealth creation. Only a little over seventy-five years ago women did not have the right to vote as full-fledged citizens. Only a little over fifty years ago women were moved out of higher-paying manufacturing jobs to lower-paying secretarial/clerical jobs with the return of World War II veterans. Only a little over forty years ago women could still be legally paid less for doing exactly the same work in the same types of positions as men. Pregnant women have been legally protected from job discrimination for less than thirty years. Equitable funding for women's sports, an arena for building team leadership skills, is less than thirty years old. The strong encouragement of women in management and other professions is less than twenty years old. The effects of such inequality are not erased overnight; and even when the legal status of women has formally changed, many years must transpire until the results of such change trickle down to real and substantial effects on most organizations. Because the effects of these shifts will be felt in organizations for decades to come, all male and female leaders must come to grips with them.

However, at the same time, it is important for female managers who become senior organizational leaders to recognize their changing positions within the organization. If such women hope to make a broad contribution to the common organizational life, they must shift from a mentality of struggle for women to one of leadership responsibility for all whom they lead, male and female. Such leaders cannot afford to see themselves or to be seen as advocates for one sex to the detriment of the other sex. Doing so would violate standards of fairness and equity in most organizations; and these values, which judge people by their merit, not their sex, are the very ones for which women leaders have argued in their own struggle for advancement to senior responsibilities.

Finally, despite some pockets of resistance, Western models of gender relations in organizations are being exported globally. While we acknowledge historical inequalities in the United States, the gulf between the cultural and legal positioning of men and women is far greater in many other countries. The gendered culture created in Western corporate organizations is being transported around the world, gradually informing the interactions of men and women in both work and broader social settings. The effect of this cultural transfer could be major. Thus, for the sake of global relations we must take responsibility for what we are exporting.

Organization-formative Faith

For these reasons alone, leaders must become adept at weaving healthy gender relations into their organizational cultures. However, beyond these practical considerations for attending to the interactions of men and women within organizations, leaders who embrace Christian perspectives have unique reasons for creating a healthy fabric of gender and organizational culture. Management professionals should care about the intersection of gender and organizational life because world-formative Christian faith requires it.

What do I mean in suggesting that a world-formative faith should spur us to action regarding gender concerns? To understand this thesis first requires one to understand and adopt a world-formative faith. What is it?

World-formative faith embraces personal Christian piety. It is faith in a personal God who expects communion, gratitude, and faithfulness from believers in Christ's promises. It is not a faith which divorces our human relationships with God from our visions for human relationships to others and to the culture; but without the establishment and continuous nurture of this personal commitment, motivations and decisions easily run amuck. Without such, our senses of social responsibility and organizational ethics too easily become hollow shells of questionable motivation.

In addition, world-formative faith includes Christian thinking. To be profoundly Christian and thoroughly effective, managerial professionals must understand the theological and social assumptions underlying their leadership. In that regard they must understand the discussions of calling, identity, and community explored in earlier sections of this work: the scriptural concept of vocation as the divine/human connection, not first as a matter of gender; the differentiation between a scriptural model of human identity informed by sex and a contemporary model completely based on it; and the New Testament church community as the model for our organizational communities where talents committed to a meaningful purpose, not gender, provide the basis on which organizational relationships develop. World-formative faith requires careful exegesis, hard thinking, and informed learning about all such ideas.

Yet Christian piety and thinking are only two of the three components of a world-formative faith. The third element of such faith is the drive to structurally and culturally loosen the hold of sin over the created order. This part of faith acknowledges that life as we know it does not match our Creator's intent. The goodness of creation continues to be corroded by sin; in that context, we have an obligation of obedience to alter the structures and cultures of this world so they more closely conform to God's intent. This third element of world-formative faith applies to the structures and cultures of our organizations.[28] In that context, world-formative faith becomes organization-formative faith.

Developing organization-formative faith is not easy. It must be cultivated with an acknowledgment of organizational sin, a concept not popularized in organizational circles. Leaders may admit to misjudgments, miscalculations, misinterpretations, or mistakes. However, they don't talk about the possibility of organizational sin.

Yet sin is a pervasive force in all areas of the cosmos, including organizations. It is the opposite of the *shalom* which God promises in the Scriptures, the "universal flourishing, wholeness, and delight—a rich state of affairs in which natural needs are satisfied and natural gifts fruitfully employed."[29] Sin is the absence of right relationships in an ethical community; it involves interactions that have been wounded by the absence of justice.[30] Any area of organizational life in which we see a picture of less perfect *shalom* is affected by sin. It is not what God intended and not the way life is supposed to be.

Gender relations in the workplace are one such area in which the relationships between men and women all too frequently are not what God intended. They do not reflect *shalom*, the created order in which males and females were both accorded dignity and respect as images of God, in which both were given responsibility for the development and care of creation, and in which male/female relationships reflected mutual help and companionship.

Instead, gender-related sin in organizations comes in many forms. At times it is an obvious sin of commission. Deliberate attempts to sexually intimidate through touch, language, pictures, or innuendo are clear violations of workplace wholeness. However, the office romance for which both parties volunteer can also be such sin. Commitments to spouses can erode through close unguarded interactions of a man and woman working and traveling together. In both cases organizations should think carefully about whether they allow or even foster such sin.

However, just as frequently, gender-related sin is the sin of omission. It is the values that leaders could have expressed, the policy initiatives that they could have begun, the reward systems for managers that they could have constructed. Each of these could have created an organization in which men and women were more equally valued and treated. The sin occurs when such changes are not introduced.

Why do leaders who embrace Christian principles allow gender-related inequality and injustice to remain in the organizations which they lead? Likely there are many reasons. For some, this is a matter of ignorance. They have not cultivated a biblical vision for social structures and relationships that differ from those of their own experience and the natural affinity and understanding of one's own sex. They are content with a particular model for gender relations which, similarly to race relations, grows from a "vast historical and cultural matrix that includes traditions, old patterns of relationships and behavior, atmospheres of expectations, social habits."[31] In such circumstances leaders are not to blame for what they have inherited but must still take responsibility for the attitudes and understandings they maintain.

Other leaders allow gender-related inequality and injustice to remain because of their relative priorities, given human limitations

71

on time and resources. They have decided, either consciously or unconsciously, that other concerns are simply more pressing: timely production, prompt customer service, a new acquisition, rising dividends per share, preventing kickbacks, the ethics of the cash drawer, race relations, community responsibility, or something else. These other concerns all do matter, both to the survival of the organization and the strength of its contribution to the *shalom* that God intended. Yet the voice of those who have struggled because of differentiated treatment based on their sex should be joined with these other legitimate concerns.

Unfortunately, for still other faith-based leaders, sin makes us, both female and male, unwilling to risk our status to champion the cause of those who have suffered organizational injustice because of their sex. We are afraid that our efforts will be misperceived. We are afraid that we will be identified as obstructionists instead of loyalists, as whiners instead of team players. This is a difficult issue that may involve substantial career risks for men and women who champion gender justice. We sometimes become afraid to sacrifice our personal standing for the good of others; so we back away.

However, leaders who are serious about a Christian faith that is world-formative must address gender relations in the workplace along with other concerns. Why? Because, if, for these leaders, world-formative faith means organization-formative faith, then Christian gender relations are important for the universal flourishing which we must work to create in organizational life. We have many other responsibilities to which we must attend; but, given the history of twentieth-century gender relations and the place of women and men in the twenty-first-century global economy, addressing gender in the workplace is critical to the organizational and global *shalom* we are called to build.

Building the Workplace Culture

Assuming that we accept responsibility for overcoming organizational sins related to gender, what are the specific responsibilities of senior leaders? Amid the host of books, articles, TV talk shows, consultants, and seminars proffering advice about gender in the workplace, to what should we attend?

It is quite likely that every decision and process in an organization's life is affected by questions of gender, either directly or indirectly. Yet, given the infinite variety of human interactions in an organization's world, an attempt to catalog that decision list would be endless. Doing so may actually divert attention from a larger organizational paradigm within which we should view the intersection of gender and organizational life. We could lose sight of the forest by looking at all the trees. Furthermore, an attempt to provide answers to specific gender-related conundrums is fruitless apart from a careful analysis of specific organizational contexts. There are always multiple factors that must be weighed along with gender; and unique organizational values, histories, actors, and environments must be taken into account. Recommendations about specific organizational questions given in a vacuum are not helpful.

However, in a broader frame for organizational thinking and doing, leaders have at least four areas of duty related to gender. Our responsibilities include the personal values we model, the organizational structures we develop, the decision processes we honor, and the vision for living within which we shape the organization's ethos.

First, the personal conduct of senior leaders on gender-related issues does matter. Our character and the resulting behavior affect organizational life. We may espouse access, equity, fairness, and opportunity for both sexes in the workplace; but who will take the message seriously if our own behavior exemplifies that of a "Queen Bee" or "Lion King"? If we are more focused on building our own territories than enriching opportunities for others, why should our statements about gender concern be treated as more than window dressing?

What aspects of personal conduct affect the credibility of senior leaders in the workplace? One powerful piece of the model is the relationship of senior leaders to their own spouses and families. While the nature of specific roles will vary, it is difficult to trust a leader who expresses concern for fairness, equity, and dignity in workplace gender relations when that person has not exhibited similar personal concern. No marriage is perfect, and families can be troubled by dynamics not of their own choosing. However, senior leaders who honor their spouses and families, giving them the time and respect they rightfully deserve, will be seen as more trustworthy on the issue of gender relations in the workplace.

Actual conduct of senior leaders in the work environment is another powerful piece of the personal model. It is the behavior exhibited not only toward peers but also toward administrative assistants and secretaries. Clearly sexual intimidation is out of bounds. However, senior leaders are also models when they make sure that the voices of both sexes are heard in corporate meetings or when they pointedly mentor a male or female who may be stymied by a sense of organizational discrimination. Their modeling may involve sincere inquiries into the career aspirations of those in jobs heavily sex-stereotyped, or "thank yous" expressed without coercion on Secretary's Day. Since gender is a highly personal matter, a senior leader's personal story and conduct will greatly affect credibility on gender-related concerns.

Second, if we are serious about influencing the long-term culture of our organizations, the responsibilities of senior leaders must extend beyond personal modeling. They involve the development of organizational structures and processes which foster gender-related equity and harmony. Structures will involve the consideration of every aspect of human resource development and use. They will include policies for recruitment and selection of new employees, issues of job design and job placement, structures for compensation, training, career development, and even retirement. These are critical, organization-formative forces on issues of gender.

Some of these structures are matters of law. For example, the Equal Pay Act of 1963 and Title VII of the 1965 Civil Rights Act make it illegal to discriminate on the basis of gender, race, or ethnic origin in matters of recruitment, selection, compensation, and the provision of opportunity. Yet these laws provide only the minimal floor for our efforts to create organizational *shalom* in the workplace. They do not require an organization to redesign, enabling job sharing, flex time, contract work, or the home office as possibilities for working parents desiring flexibility with their children. Laws do not require that human resource offices consider the relative equity of compensation between different job classes, some of which are heavily dominated by one sex or the other. Government regulations cannot overcome the double standard of evaluation, divided by gender, which often assumes the ability of men and yet requires proof of the ability of women. Laws do not require that organizational evaluation systems reward time spent mentoring men or women who are struggling to develop their path in an organization.

Leaders who take world-formative faith seriously should recognize that the legal requirements regarding gender only go the first mile. However, going the second, and even the third mile will be required to create organizational *shalom*, that universal flourishing where humans opportunities to work come because of gifts, interests, and developed competence which are not thwarted by structural barriers in the organization.

Yet organizational structures alone do not build universal flourishing. Accompanying decision processes comprise the third element that must be reviewed. It is often in the process of real decision making that the "rubber hits the road" on matters of gender. Structures and policies cannot address every organizational decision and the role of gender in that process. Despite those conscious formulations, ongoing decisions reflect what and how things are really done.

What responsibilities might senior leaders have for such processes when decisions are made by a host of actors on the organizational scene? Is significant influence possible? Granted, leaders don't make every organizational decision. They do, however, assert the values and set the tone for organizational decision making. That tone is influenced by the questions they ask in the drive toward decision closure. They can speed up or slow down a process when gender-related issues are at stake. A more rapid process may be supported to recruit a candidate of opposite gender who balances out the needs of the team. A slower process may honor a variety of voices, allowing both males and females to have appropriate input into decisions that affect them and their families.

Evaluating decision processes is challenging. There will be times when the results of a decision are attributed to the chasm between the sexes, even when such is not the case. Promotion of the male instead of the female may be reasonable and just, given the requirements of the position and the attributes of the individuals vying for the opportunity. There may be nothing sexist about that choice and nothing which the senior leader reasonably ought to question. Yet that decision may also reflect subconscious concerns about whether the female applicant, by virtue of being female, can handle the responsibility; and such perceptions ought to be questioned.

Monitoring decision processes is not easy. Doing so requires senior leaders to cultivate the integrity of other decision makers and to sort carefully through organizational decisions which may be influenced by gender. Leaders must recognize the potential effects of double standards, of perceptual bias, of gender dynamics on work teams dominated by one sex—all to determine when the dignity of either sex has been assaulted or when the claim of assault is false. We must also teach other decision makers to carefully monitor their choices, thinking and talking together about when sex-based differences should matter and when they should not.

Leaders must then teach those with whom they associate how to work through remaining gender-related conflicts and value forgiveness in organizational decisions. Even if organization men and women are intent on creating organizational *shalom*, differences in perception, poor timing, the press of other external forces, and imperfect communication continue to hamper its development. A man's many years of loyal commitment are disregarded. A woman's potential is overlooked. A woman's early exit from a meeting is attributed to lack of commitment instead of child care constraints. A man's reasonable decision to hire another male associate is seen as necessarily sexist.

These sins create the gulfs that separate men and women from their work and from each other, barriers that are not the way it's supposed to be. Leaders who value organization-formative faith must expect authenticity in dealing with such concerns openly and honestly. They need to remind organization women and men that gender-based shortcomings should be acknowledged and forgiveness sought from those whose contributions have been thwarted. Leaders must also encourage the recipients of gender-related injustice to forgive seventy times seven, the infinite measure described by Jesus in Matthew 18:22. Acknowledgment of responsibility and corresponding forgiveness can free both the perpetrator of gender-related wrong and the victim for a future together. What leaders teach about handling the fallout of decisions is critical in creating organizational cultures that flourish appropriately.

Finally, leaders who believe Christian faith should influence the workplace must integrate the broader rhythms of living with the syncopations of the organization. Organizations that constantly push the limits of human capacity for work exacerbate gender-related problems when employees are prevented from finding personal time, meeting obligations to spouses and children for extended periods, or become isolated from broader communities of need. When the need for "Sabbath time" is ignored, gender-based frustrations rise.

The New Testament basis for "Sabbath time" is grace instead of law; but the purposes for Sabbath should still be honored. These purposes are, first, an opportunity for celebration, delight and renewal in God, and second, an opportunity to exercise community responsibility. Organizations that honor the concept of "Sabbath time" soften the edge of gender-related frustrations. [32]

There must be a rhythm of organizational time which allows all members, both male and female, to reflect on and refill their spiritual and emotional bank accounts. Steven Covey documents this need in *The Seven Habits of Highly Effective People*, arguing that if organizations truly expect peak performance from men and women, these people must have time to "sharpen the saw" of their own calling and personal mission with their God, within themselves, and with their families, friends, and communities. [33] When there is time to reflect and interact with others as a man or a woman outside the work environment, a reaffirmed personal identity can provide renewal and new strength for coping with organizational life.

However, leaders must also allow organizational members to take community needs seriously; this is the second reason for "Sabbath time." [34] In the United States many of those needs are met through volunteerism. Organizations must recognize that the framework of community social services historically directed by volunteer women is deteriorating as more women enter the paid labor force. If community volunteerism is to continue as part of our obligation for the poor, the alien, and the fatherless, organizations will need to consider how such volunteerism can be incorporated into their organizational rhythms.

Human beings must be bigger than the roles they occupy as organization women and men. If leaders believe in organization-formative faith, then they must appropriately honor life beyond the boundaries of the organization.

Senior leaders will not find it easy to build organizational *shalom* in a gender-sensitive world. Through personal modeling, organizational structure, decision processes, and allowance for broad human development, leaders must try to cultivate wholeness. Yet developing workplace cultures which honor equally the needs and aspirations of both men and women, while simultaneously serving customers and other stakeholders, is a difficult undertaking.

However, an organization's culture is the arena of impact for managerial leaders wishing to express a world-formative Christian faith. World-formative faith becomes real in organizational life as we strive to recreate the *shalom* of the created order. In that order, as male and female, we worked together with perfect complementarity. Beginning this re-creation is the realm of our responsibility.

Conclusion: Out to Whatever the Future Holds

By deliberate design God created humans female and male. While each was given gifts and responsibilities before God, we were created to live and work as sex-differentiated creatures in this time and place. This difference was meant to provide human complementarity. It was not intended as a limitation on our callings, our leadership, or our organizational cultures. Yet gender became such a limitation under the crushing weight of sin; and now we live in a post-Fall world where the broken and perverted aspirations of females and males play out each day in the workplace culture.

Yet we also live between the times, between the Resurrection and the Second Coming. While society is sometimes called post-Christian, we really live somewhere in the middle of the Christian era; and so we must continue to have the "conviction of things not seen" (Heb. 11:1). By faith we know that the evils and frustrations we experience in the relationships of organization men and women are not the way things are suppose to be. By faith we know that while organizational good and evil run their side-by-side course, gender-related evil is already programmed to lose.

Therefore, as men and women who lead, we run the race before us, working out the gratitude that comes from grace. We are faithful to our callings in both paid and unpaid roles. We aspire to leadership that changes us and allows us to change others. We work to shape organizational cultures that reflect our world-formative faith, creating access, equity, and opportunity for all women and men at work. There are moments of promise for both now and the future; and we celebrate the progress that is possible.

Still, we see in a glass darkly. Between the times some mysteries about sexual difference and their effects on organizational life will never be fully understood. Attempts to build organizational *shalom* are thwarted by incomplete knowledge, imperfect information, insensitivity, dishonesty, time constraints, and a host of other forces. The pain we experience does not easily subside, and the forgiveness we seek is hard to find.

This is life between the times; but when human time ends, we can lay our burdens down. The organizational synergy of which we dream and for which we work, that perfect *shalom* in which females and males flourish together in a harmony of calling, leadership, and culture, will come. This is no utopian myth.

Then each of us, female and male, organization woman and organization man, can be whole before the great "I Am." The pain of gender brokenness in our lives can pass away, replaced forever by perfect unity with each other and with God everlasting. Toward this end we work and believe.

Chapter 2

Feminist Theological Reflections on Justice and Solidarity with Women Workers

Barbara Hilkert Andolsen

In this essay, I will examine facets of gender in organizational life different from those helpfully illuminated by Shirley Roels. I will give more attention to the situation of the majority of women workers, who are clerical and service workers, not managers. This response stresses a social ethical approach to the issue of gender in organizations. Such an approach sets ethical questions in a larger social context. It seeks to understand how an interlocking set of social institutions shapes the contours of our moral choices.

This essay will be unabashedly feminist, i.e., the well-being of women will be a central moral criterion throughout this essay. The radically equal human dignity of women provides a touchstone here. No genuine common good for women and men is possible unless women's well-being is taken with moral seriousness equal to that accorded to men's welfare. In addition, a commitment to the equal dignity of women is consistent with fundamental Christian convictions.

In this brief essay I cannot provide a full overview of the theological ethical themes that are relevant to the situation of "pink-collar" workers. Therefore, I have selected three concepts particularly germane to this discussion: justice, solidarity, and social sin.

Justice

Justice is a central moral virtue that provides a basic framework to describe what persons owe to one another as fellow human beings. As the United States Catholic bishops say, "the norms of basic justice state the minimum levels of mutual care and respect that all persons and communities owe to each other in our imperfect world."[1] Justice requires that the fundamental structures of a society be organized in such a way that fair treatment is provided for every member of that society.

An important aspect of justice is "distributive" justice. This aspect of justice is concerned with morally evaluating the patterns of distribution of goods and benefits among members of a social group. For example, in the United States, well-paying jobs are social "goods" which are unevenly distributed among various groups in society. Men hold more of the high-paying jobs than do women. Non-Hispanic Whites hold more high-paying jobs than do African Americans, Native Americans, or Hispanics. Thus, the distribution of managerial and professional jobs in the United States raises questions concerning distributive justice.

There is no single standard of distributive justice that usefully specifies how every type of social "good" ought to be rightfully distributed. For example, in an advanced economy, basic medical care ought to be justly distributed to every member of society who *needs* medical care. A managerial job, on the other hand, is not the sort of "good" that is appropriately distributed based entirely on "need." It is morally appropriate to take qualifications (or "merit") into account when "distributing" a particular managerial position, if qualifications are fairly defined. However, a "fair" definition of qualifications for a position is more difficult to achieve than is often understood. The danger that gender expectations or other unfair cultural stereotypes will prejudice the selection process is a morally significant problem. Roels has given us a concrete instance of this with her example of the woman with younger children applying for the leadership position.

A key recent understanding of justice conceives it as participation. According to this perspective, all members of a group have both the right and responsibility to be active participants contributing to the common good of society. In the economic realm, justice as participation does not necessarily mean that society should be designed so that all adults hold paying positions. One can be an active participant in the economic life of society through domestic or volunteer activities, too.

If justice entails participation, then marginalization is a sign of injustice. This resonates with the biblical emphasis on justice as involving special concern for the well-being of the poor and the socially vulnerable—for fatherless children, widows, and resident aliens. In the Hebrew Scriptures, justice for the poor was an obligatory response to Yahweh's action in bringing the chosen people out of slavery in Egypt.

At the center of the message of Jesus of Nazareth was the kingdom of God in which those who hunger and thirst for justice would be satisfied. Jesus declared that, at the Final Judgment, people would be judged according to their treatment of the hungry, prisoners, and strangers (Matt. 25:31-46). All are called to participate in the kingdom of God. Christians cannot bring about the fullness of the kingdom solely through their own efforts. Still, they are called—in every aspect of life (including organizational life)—to create greater opportunities for the marginalized to participate in the life of the community.

Indeed, a central question concerning the treatment of women in organizations is: Have women have been marginalized and, hence, unjustly treated? Or, are women clustered in different, but still fairly distributed, organizational positions? If women as a group have different psychological characteristics that lead them to find satisfaction in performing different tasks, it is no injustice to assign women to different organizational positions. On this question, I agree with Roels who rejects a theory of gender complementarity that postulates differences in male and female psychological traits that are somehow rooted in biological differences between the sexes. Roels makes a crucial point when she challenges notions of innate gender difference that "run roughshod over individual differences in both men and women." I especially appreciate her cautions about too ready acceptance of theories about a feminine style of management that women would "naturally" bring with them to managerial positions.

Solidarity

Solidarity is a virtue that supports justice by giving us a keen awareness of the moral bonds that tie us to other human beings. In the encyclical *Sollicitudo Rei Socialis* ("On Social Concern"), Pope John Paul II defines solidarity as "*a firm and persevering determination* to commit oneself to the *common good*; that is to say to the good of all and of each individual."[2] Solidarity requires special solicitude for those whose social vulnerabilities place them at greater risk of exploitation, deprivation, and suffering.

Solidarity involves a recognition that all human beings are interrelated as fellow members of the human race. People are increasingly bound together by their participation in a global economy and their dependence on an intricately interrelated natural environment.

Christians find this theme in the doctrines of creation, redemption and sanctification. All human beings, male and female, have worth as creatures of the one Creator. Further, in and through Jesus, Sophia-Spirit has reconciled all humanity with Herself and with one another. This same Sophia-Spirit is God's continuing presence among us, sustaining us in the often difficult journey toward God's kingdom of justice, wholeness, and *shalom* for all as God's people.

Thus, a Christian understanding of solidarity arises in part from the awareness that all human beings share a life affirming relationship with Sophia-Spirit. I realize that many Christian readers will not be familiar with the term Sophia-Spirit that I am using here to name what we have traditionally called the Holy Spirit. Many readers will also have been jolted by my description of Sophia-Spirit reconciling humankind with "Herself." Sophia-Spirit is a feminine, biblical image for God that has been lifted up by several contemporary feminist theologians.[3]

Another translation of Sophia is Wisdom. In the Hebrew Scriptures, God is sometimes personified as Wisdom going among Her people to promote justice. In Proverbs 8, Wisdom leads the people on the "path of justice"; She allows lawgivers to "establish justice" (Prov. 8:15, 20). Scripture scholar Elisabeth Schüssler Fiorenza contends that some Jewish followers of Jesus of Nazareth understood his ministry and the significance of his death and resurrection in light of contemporaneous Jewish spiritual traditions that focused on Sophia. She says that some of Jesus' contemporaries saw him—and he saw himself—as a messenger bringing good news to the poor and outcast on behalf of Divine Woman Wisdom (a Jewish image for God).[4]

It is awkward to use what may be unfamiliar female imagery for the Divine in an essay where I cannot discuss at length the sources and implications of such imagery. In particular, I cannot discuss here the danger that feminine names for God will be understood in a way that reinforces gender stereotypes. (I hope that speaking of the Divine Being as Wisdom, leading humanity on the path of justice, avoids some of the worst pitfalls of stereotypical feminine imagery.)

However, I contend that using feminine Christian imagery for the Divine is important for two reasons. First, I want to echo (in a distinctive way) Roels's theological anchoring of women's equal moral worth in the theological doctrine of women as created "in the image and likeness of God." If women are made in the image of God, then it is fitting sometimes to speak of God in womanly terms.

Second, there are important connections between the language that we use to speak of the Divine and the human patterns of authority with which we are culturally comfortable. If male imagery and language dominate our thought and speech about God, then we will be more comfortable with men in positions of power and authority and less comfortable when women assume those positions. Conversely, if we are committed to striving for a society in which women share power and authority equally with men, then we need a multiplicity of images to describe the Ultimate Power in the universe—female images as well as male images. Divine Woman Wisdom is one image available to Christian (and Jewish) women and men who strive to follow Her path toward justice for women (and men) in every sort of organization.

Social Sin

Sin names the perennial human tendency to make evil choices in our lives as individuals, groups (including organizations), and societies. Both Roels and I find sin a concept that must be explored when analyzing the relationships between women and men in contemporary organizations. Individual or personal sin is a deliberate personal choice to do something morally wrong. Social sin names the evil that we do when we cooperate with and perpetuate patterns of evil in our *common life*. The sins of one generation deform its cultural traditions and its social institutions and mar the social heritage of the next generation. Individuals in the next generation find themselves enmeshed in sinful situations that they did not personally create or choose. Surrounded by structures of sin, their moral sensitivities are dulled and their will to end social injustices is weakened. Social sin often involves an element of "moral blindness." The sinners are inattentive to the human harms that result from taken-for-granted structures of sin.

Language can be an element in the structures of sin. Harms for which there is no language—no name—cannot be subjected to that social critique that is a crucial element in the moral transformation of structures of sin. For example, vulnerable workers have always been at risk of sexual exploitation by those with economic power.

When Catharine A. MacKinnon created a legal term to name this form of exploitation—sexual harassment—she broke the social silence surrounding this harassment, allowing us to analyze it and to create new social structures to reduce it.

Ethicist Mary Pellauer talks about the formation of a "moral callus" that makes us thick skinned, ethically speaking.[5] Such a moral callus protects the subject from painful empathy aroused when we squarely face the suffering of the oppressed. Ensnared by a variety of social evils, including racism and sexism, we go about our daily tasks—both personal or organizational—calloused to the injustices around us.

Gender and Race in the Management Sector

Roels has provided a stimulating look at gender primarily at the managerial level of organizational life. I have some additional questions about race, gender, and management.

In the last two decades, women have made very substantial progress in obtaining a fair share of management positions, at least at the lower levels. Women now hold managerial positions proportionate to their overall share in the labor force. Nevertheless, a "glass ceiling" still prevents proportional movement into the upper echelons of executives. Women make up only 3 to 5 percent of executives at the level of vice president or above. Even the best-prepared women are far from achieving success equal to that of men. For example, researchers followed the careers of male and female graduates from Stanford University Business School in 1982. Ten years later, only 2 percent of the women had risen to the rank of chief executive officer, president, or chairman of a company, compared with 16 percent of their male classmates. One in ten women had reached the level of vice president; almost one in four men held that title.[6]

Moreover, *white* women have made the most significant inroads into managerial positions. In 1994, 13 percent of European American women who worked for wages held executive, administrative, and managerial jobs. Nine percent of African American women earning wages held comparable jobs. Eight percent of Hispanic women wage-earners were in that occupational category.[7] Minority women hold less than 1 percent of all senior executive slots. Examining the fact that minority women are not getting fair opportunities to obtain *professional and managerial* jobs is crucial, because such jobs are now one of the *fastest growing* segments of the labor market.

The key variable in getting a foothold on the managerial career ladder is a strong educational background. However, children from differing social classes (both female and male) have very different access to quality education. Women from the middle and upper classes who pursue the appropriate education will probably continue to find positions, at least in the lower levels of management.

Over the last decade African American young people have been more likely to get a college degree, but they still lag behind Caucasians and Asian-Pacific Americans in the proportions of young adults who have college degrees. The picture is less bright when looking at Native Americans and Hispanics. Only about one in ten workers from those groups has a college degree. The ethical principles of justice and solidarity should lead us to be very concerned that certain young people do not get the education that is a prerequisite to getting a good job, such as a management position.

My discussion of competition for managerial jobs might seem to imply that I view the labor market as one large, level playing field on which all female laborers and all male laborers compete to obtain better positions. However, I do not accept the model of today's "labor market" as a single market. Rather, I agree with labor economists who, examining gender and racial differences in occupational groups, have insisted that there are several labor markets containing jobs with different types of wages and benefits, job duties, and job security.

To understand the ways in which different groups are channeled into different types of jobs, I have found particularly helpful a book by Barbara Reskin and Patricia Roos, *Job Queues, Gender Queues.* The authors describe the process of allocating jobs as a process that involves a reciprocal ordering of preferences by employers and applicants. Employers maintain a labor queue that ranks potential employees from the most desirable to the least desirable or unacceptable. Job seekers, in turn, have a job queue in which they rank the jobs realistically available to them from the most desirable to the least desirable or unacceptable. Employers are influenced in their ordering process by some noneconomic, cultural considerations. In fact, Reskin and Roos contend "most labor queues are so overwhelmingly ordered by sex that they are essentially gender queues."[8] William Julius Wilson cites interviews showing that labor queues are ordered by race and ethnicity, as well as gender.[9] African American males from

87

the inner city are relegated to the bottom of the labor queue by suburban employers.

Most women workers compete for jobs in the secondary labor market—lower-paying jobs, more routine duties, less chance for career advancement, modest job security in these "dead-end" positions. A significant number of women are relegated to the tertiary labor market—low wages, no benefits, onerous duties, and no job security. This aspect of contemporary employment patterns is not the focus of Roels's essay, but it is the reality for many. Thus, the remainder of my response will concentrate on women in clerical and service jobs.

Issues Concerning Clerical Workers

Most women who work for organizations are clerical and service workers. Partly because of the computerization of offices, over the last several decades, clerical jobs have been changing in complex ways. They are being transformed in ways that have differing implications for the welfare and the dignity of particular groups of women workers. I shall give examples from the insurance industry, which employs many clerical workers as quasi-production workers, although other illustrations could also be used. Computers and telecommunications technologies have allowed insurance companies to redesign clerical jobs to enhance efficiency and ultimately profitability. Most insurance companies have pursued one of two patterns. (Sometimes, the same company has used the first of these models to handle high-volume lines of business and the second in more specialized lines of insurance.)

The first style of computerized clerical work is organized to produce a high-volume, uniform output. For example, clerks enter standard data from applications into a computer system. Computers are programmed to analyze the data, issue the policy, generate a premium notice, and pay the agent's commission. The same computer system may be programmed automatically to monitor the number of applications that a clerk processes, the speed at which she completes them, and her accuracy rate.

In other facilities, clerical workers handle a group of clients, interacting by phone with the customers or insurance agents directly. The computer performs routine underwriting tasks; the remaining tasks require flexibility and human judgment. Because the remaining clerical tasks require judgment, the work is less easily subjected to computer monitoring. However, some elements of the work, such as the time it takes to answer a phone call, may be monitored.

The second category of clerical jobs involves more challenging work with greater task variety. Such clerical work provides more opportunity to exercise judgment. Sometimes clerical workers make decisions that, in the past, were made by professional underwriters. However, clerical decision-making power under the second model should not be exaggerated. Management usually sets parameters on the discretion that these more advanced clerical workers can exercise. Nevertheless, they have increased responsibility; but, too often, the clerical worker is not compensated with higher wages.

These differing patterns for the redesign of clerical work give workers disparate chances to develop their God-given talents while on the job. Roels, in discussing the religious concept "vocation," talked about the individual's responsibility to use his or her unique gifts in a fashion mindful of God's will for human life. I would add that organizations have a moral responsibility to seek, where possible, to design jobs in a way that gives employees enlarged opportunities to cultivate their talents. I join Roels in envisioning workplaces where workers "gifts, interests and developed competence" are not "thwarted"; rather, they are enhanced. The choices that managers are making about the design of clerical jobs shape clerical workers' opportunities to use their God-given talents more fully.

I want to mention briefly another managerial decision about clerical jobs that has a crucial impact on opportunities for urban women, often women of color, to use their God-given talents in the workplace. Many clerical jobs are being relocated to the suburbs, rural areas, or even foreign countries. Many managers, who are seeking workers to perform routine clerical duties, have decided that they can get more skilled workers at lower cost by hiring workers in suburban and rural locations.

When managers no longer believe that urban school systems can provide a well-educated labor force, suburban locations, smaller cities, and even foreign countries look good to corporate decision makers.[10] Clerical jobs in urban centers in the United States have provided important employment opportunities for women of color. Justice and solidarity are violated by the displacement of jobs away from central cities and the abandonment of the women workers who live there.

Contingent Labor

Contingent work is another workplace issue that has important implications for women workers in clerical and service occupations. Contingent jobs do not have many positive features of standard jobs. A standard job is a full-time position that offers basic benefits such as health care coverage and a pension plan, is covered by protective labor legislation, and offers long-term employment if the worker's performance remains satisfactory.

Contingent work involves less mutual commitment from employer and employee. Among the forms of contingent work are employee leasing, workers supplied by temporary agencies, and independent contractors hired for particular projects. Throughout the industrialized world, women and men from socially disadvantaged ethnic groups make up the bulk of the contingent labor force.

I am asking whether a human resource strategy that divides workers into a core work force that is offered standard jobs and a peripheral group of contingent workers contradicts solidarity and threatens to create new structures of sin in the labor market(s). Does the practice of employing growing numbers of contingent workers represent a spreading pattern of morally disturbing marginalization?

Managers are using more contingent workers because contingent work gives management greater control of labor costs. Some temporary workers receive lower wages than full-time employees. Companies do not have to pay high health care premiums or make pension contributions for most contingent employees. When management decides that cutting labor costs is prudent, contingent workers are dismissed easily.

On the contingent worker's side, such arrangements allow students to find temporary jobs during summer break or part-time work that suits their class schedules. Vigorous older people can supplement their retirement incomes through contingent work. Women with families can coordinate flexible hours of paid employment with domestic responsibilities.

Some contingent work arrangements give workers an opportunity to combine work with other endeavors. However, since the employer has greater bargaining power than an individual employee, flexibility is often defined in ways that benefit the employer, not the employee. For example, the company using a temporary help agency specifies the hours the "temp" works and the duration of the assignment. The temporary help agency offers a temporary worker the assignment on the terms set forth by the agency's customer. The temp has the flexibility to accept the assignment or reject it. If she accepts it, she is usually bound by the hours and dates the customer requested. In addition, the counselors at the temporary help agency are interested in filling the customer's request with qualified temps as expeditiously as possible. If a potential temp rejects multiple offers because they do not fit the temp's preferred pattern of days and times, then the counselor is likely to call first other temps who are more "flexible" about accepting assignments. Thus, the flexibility that many temps gain is limited, or even illusory.

Roels praises job sharing, flex-time, and telecommuting because such workplace flexibility allows working parents more easily to accommodate the needs of their children. Flex-time arrangements where workers can opt for schedules that more adequately fit their family responsibilities *are* helpful to families. Steady, part-time work also gives many workers, who *voluntarily* elect to work a reduced work week, more time to attend to family chores. However, other types of contingent work are difficult for families because they involve unpredictable workplace demands. For example, as hospitals are restructuring, more nurses work on a contingent basis. A nurse in that situation may receive short notice of an opening. If that nurse has younger children, arranging for good, stable child care may be difficult when her schedule is so unpredictable.

Other adverse consequences are associated with contingent labor. Such jobs often do not include important fringe benefits such as health care and pension coverage. A contingent worker may not receive paid sick leave. Contingent workers are rarely eligible for corporate training programs. Temporary workers or independent contractors do not have an opportunity to move up the corporate job ladder.

Justice and solidarity should prompt us to be uneasy with the growing use of contingent workers throughout most of the industrialized world. We need to ask whether social sin contributes to a pattern in which women and men from minority groups make up a disproportionate share of the contingent work force.

Gender, Organizational Duties, and Family Responsibilities

Since the early 1980s, over half the mothers with young children have been working for wages. The average married woman who is

91

employed full-time puts in a 65-hour week when work and household labor are both taken into account.[11] Men are also doing more housework than they did several decades earlier. However, husbands spend only about 50 percent of the time doing housework that their wives spend.

The distribution of work between husband and wife in the home is reciprocally interrelated with women's positions in other organizations. Most women working for wages are still employed in clerical and service positions and in traditionally feminine professions that pay relatively low wages. More men are employed in manufacturing, technical, professional, and managerial positions that pay relatively high wages. If the husband is the higher wage earner, subordinating the wife's job to the family's domestic needs is economically rational. In a vicious cycle, a woman's disproportionate family responsibilities make her seem a less reliable, less committed worker. So, women get fewer demanding, high-paying jobs. Then women, as secondary wage earners, choose to subordinate their jobs to their family responsibilities, and the cycle starts again.

What is needed for women to achieve equality in the workplace is more than "family friendly" organizational policies, such as flextime schedules, although those are valuable contributions to family well-being and, therefore, the common good. If seemingly gender-neutral policies like parental leave are used predominantly by women, women will continue to suffer organizational disadvantages. Some managers will be reluctant to assign women who are pregnant or have young children to key assignments, because such women may take parental leave at a time detrimental to the company's project. If the company provides paid parental leaves and this benefit is used almost exclusively by women, then young women of child bearing age will be potentially more costly employees.

It is instructive to consider what happened when the Swedish government required all employers to provide generous parental leave benefits (open to both fathers and mothers). Men rarely took any parental leave when a child was born or adopted. If a father did take a leave, it was typically for a brief time. Swedish labor union leaders reported that employers covertly discriminated against women of child-bearing age. Thus, parental leaves taken primarily by women are a mixed blessing for women.

In order for women to be treated equally within organizations, cultural patterns of male and female behavior in the family have to change. Men need to assume equal responsibilities for child rearing and household chores. Most women (who sometime in their lives bear one or more children) will not have truly equal opportunity until the men who father children assume equal responsibility for the day-to-day care of those children. Roels and I agree that more attention must be paid by all of society's institutions, including religious bodies, to men's caregiving responsibilities within their families.

Of course, husbands and fathers have had a serious, at times onerous, responsibility as breadwinners. Many of us owe profound gratitude to our fathers for the material support they gave us and, often, our (homemaker) mothers. However, if mothers are going to have a fair opportunity in the workplaces of the future, then fathers must do more at home. Fortunately, many young men would welcome organizational policies and attitudinal changes that made it possible for them to take a larger role in caring for their children.

Moreover, balancing family responsibilities and organizational duties is not just a matter of caring for young children. Increasingly, workers have elderly parents who are going through a period when they are physically and/or mentally unable to function self-sufficiently. Elder care may be the issue that effectively challenges managers to consider more seriously how their organization can be structured to allow workers more humanely to balance family responsibilities with organizational duties. Many senior male managers had wives who stayed home while the children were young. But as more women, especially well-educated women, take paying jobs, a male executive's wife (and sisters) may not be as available to care for elderly relatives. Senior male executives may find themselves struggling to combine organizational responsibilities with filial duties and may reexamine corporate policies as a result.

Unions as a Vehicle for Social Justice

Roman Catholic social thought values those social groups that human beings create to meet a variety of legitimate human needs. Such mediating institutions stand between the individual and the state or society as a whole. Churches and synagogues, parent-teacher associations, and charitable groups are all examples of mediating organizations through which human beings enhance their lives and promote the common good. Labor unions are a type of mediating institution that needs supportive scrutiny from those concerned about justice today.

Historically, many religious groups have relied on labor unions as social structures to promote the rightful claims of workers. While religious bodies have included outspoken critics of unions and their abuses, they also see unions as key mechanisms to promote justice for workers. However, the union movement in the United States is in peril, and many religious groups have not paid enough attention to the, perhaps, fatal weakening of unions.

Union membership in the United States peaked in the 1950s at 35 percent. In 1995, unions represented only 15 percent of the work force, and only 11 percent of workers in the private sector. Union decline is an international phenomenon. The American labor movement is fighting aggressively to reverse its decline, but success is not a sure thing.

Effective union representation for women workers, when it has occurred, has produced positive results. Since the dawn of industrialization in the United States, women workers have banded together to seek better wages and more control over working conditions. Women have been effective union organizers. However, women workers have faced difficulties in using unions as mediating structures to press their claims for justice on the job. Historically, the male-dominated union movement assigned lower priority to organizing women. Skilled male workers feared competition from women, because employers—who paid women workers less for doing the same work—reduced labor costs by hiring women. Some craft unions responded by banning women workers from membership.

Partly inspired by the resurgence of the feminist movement in the late 1960s, labor union women founded the Coalition of Labor Union Women (CLUW). They pressed for greater representation of women in the leadership of the union movement and greater attention to contract bargaining issues of special concern to women workers. CLUW has been an effective force for greater justice for women within the labor union movement.

Unions gain better wages for their female members. Women represented by unions earn significantly more than nonunionized women. Union membership enhances the earning power of African American and Hispanic women even more significantly than that of European American women.

The labor movement is struggling to renew itself in the United

States today. Labor leaders now understand that recruiting women workers is a key to reviving their movement. While unions have been losing ground among male workers, they are holding their own with female workers. In fact, the few unions that have been growing in size recently have done a good job in persuading women to join their ranks. In the last decade, women went from 34 percent of union membership to 40 percent.[12] Surveys show that women have more positive attitudes toward unions.

The last few years have seen a vigorous effort by the new leadership of the AFL-CIO to revitalize the labor movement. Still, currents in contemporary life are flowing against unions. Among the problems that the labor movement faces are its own reputation for corruption, a growing reliance on contingent workers who do not fit neatly into union "bargaining units," and unsupportive government policies, especially unfavorable decisions from the National Labor Relations Board.

Unions have been key mediating institutions promoting justice for workers. If the union movement atrophies beyond recovery, we will have to invent some new structure to promote justice for workers who, as individuals, are in crucial, but highly unequal, relationships with employers. The Catholic notion of social sin suggests to me that more vulnerable workers will suffer serious harms if we go through a period in which unions wither away and then are "reinvented." So I hope that, with the help of allies, including religious groups, the labor movement will renew itself now.

Concluding Remarks

Justice and solidarity bid us to be concerned about the situation of women in organizations, both as managers and as clerical, manufacturing, or service workers. The biblical notion of justice as a special concern for the socially vulnerable should make us sensitive to the marginalization of people who have poor educational opportunities or who are involuntarily trapped in contingent jobs. An appreciation of the uniqueness of each human being as a creature of God and an acknowledgment of our joint responsibility to use our talents in the service of God and neighbor ought to lead us to design jobs that challenge workers to develop their talents more fully. We also need to realign work and family responsibilities in a way that allows women to be equal participants in economic life and enables men to assume equal responsibility for dependent care. Unions have been key vehicles through which workers have achieved greater justice in the workplace. Religious groups, which have relied on unions as intermediate structures to promote justice for workers, need to join in the difficult effort to renew the labor movement, in the United States and internationally. When we work on behalf of justice for women and men in organizations, we join Divine Woman Wisdom as She leads Her people along the path of justice and solidarity in the global economy.

Chapter 3

Men and Women in Business: On Professional Ethics and the Limits of Theology

Paul F. Camenisch

Shirley Roels is clearly correct that management has undergone significant transformation in the last several decades, and Barbara Andolsen helpfully notes that such reshaping has resulted in part from the reconsideration of sex roles in the society at large. But whether Roels is correct that management has evolved into a profession is a more complex question, the answer to which depends on what one understands by "profession" or by "being a professional," and how one sees the currently dominant forms of management. An exploration of these factors will lead to a number of topics Roels raises, including the fact that Christians concerned about this society's future should surely reflect on these matters and offer their views in public debate.

One thing Christians need not do is to seek to justify women's rights to equal opportunity and to fair treatment in all sectors of the workplace. Some things by now should be quite obvious. I do not write my representatives in Washington about keeping Uzis out of the hands of children. If they need my letter, or the letters of a majority of their constituents to convince them of the need for such action, then there is a more fundamental problem which we ignore at our own peril. It will not be solved by a letter-writing campaign about Uzis. Similarly, Christians should not need to argue, for example, that women and men should receive equal pay for equal work.

All the issues involved in our discussion of women in the workplace will not be as self-evident as Florynce R. Kennedy, attorney and civil rights activist, suggested when she stated, rather graphically,

"There are very few jobs that actually require a penis or vagina. All other jobs should be open to everybody."[1] But surely the fundamental right of women to equal standing and treatment in the workplace should by now be obvious to all morally serious persons shaped by Christian ethical influences. In fact, to argue for this right may even harm the cause by implying that there are still unrefuted coherent arguments on the other side, while obscuring the deeper causes of continuing discrimination and harassment that are often immune to rational argument.

Nevertheless, the growing number of women in management is still an important opportunity for ethical reflection. Significant demographic changes in any area of a society's life—whether geographic, political, or occupational—often precipitate an examination of the lines along which that area has been and should be organized. One motive of such re-thinking is often the desire of the previously dominant group to protect what they have considered "their" territory and to preserve for themselves its privileges. Thus there is some risk in a middle-aged white male's suggestion, just as women are becoming a larger presence in the professions, or in management in particular, that we should reassess the role these occupations play in the life of the larger society. Nevertheless, the accelerating change in the gender and ethnic makeup of the professions and the attendant loosening of the control over the professions exercised by their traditionally dominant population offer an opportunity for such reconsideration that Christians, including middle-aged white males, ought not to ignore.

Society clearly stands to gain from such reconsiderations. But so do women, who otherwise may be seen—as many see the men they hope to displace—as having sold out other values such as commitment to public service and the common good for the sake of their own personal privilege and power.

Management, at least in the United States, is currently under fire for a number of reasons. The number of M.B.A.s in this country continues to multiply while plants continue to close; jobs—especially manufacturing jobs—continue to be shipped abroad; the category of temporary workers and therefore of workers without benefits continues to mushroom. Outsourcing becomes a more and more popular way of cutting some costs by passing other costs on to those less able to say no, workers desperately seeking employment. The trade deficit continues to grow, and corporations and their top management continue to be assessed on unconscionably short-term criteria; this means immediate payoffs for those who perform well according to such criteria, but raises real questions about the long-term well-being of corporations, of society, and quite possibly of the globe.

On the other hand, until very recently, at least, corporate profits were doing very well, and top management was doing and continues to do very well indeed. One group of 292 corporate executives enjoyed an average of $3.7 million in total income in 1994, receiving 187 times as much as the average worker.[2] In the 1970s that multiple was about 35.[3] The fact that the income of top CEOs in Europe and Japan is a fraction of that of CEOs in the United States would seem to pose interesting questions concerning economics, efficiency, and even justice. The fact that all such top spots in the Fortune 500 are held by males also raises issues closer to the concerns of this volume.[4]

And when ordinary folk begin to notice that in recent months the stock market is as likely to drop as to rise on news of rising employment, they rightly begin to wonder about the relation between business, especially big business where managers are more likely to claim to be professionals, and their own futures as well as society's. They then begin to understand Robert Reich when he says that the important question, now that the emerging nature of global business means that even within the same nation a rising economic tide no longer lifts all boats, is, "Are we still a society, even if we are no longer . . . [a single] economy?"[5] This more ambiguous side of the corporate life into which women are moving and of the profession of management to which they aspire must be considered along with the positive dimensions on which Roels focuses.

Assuming that management is moving toward becoming a profession, there is a second reason for women to look before they leap. The current state of the professions is not an altogether happy one. Here too we can offer only a thumbnail sketch. Because of the years of education and training involved, the public does not generally seem to begrudge such traditional professions as law and medicine the somewhat higher than average incomes they enjoy. But it is less clear to many that professionals in these fields deserve the extraordinarily high salaries that the most conspicuous among them receive. This concern is aggravated by the fact that such professionals are becoming increasingly highly specialized practitioners in areas over which they often have a monopoly, while their services are often available to ordinary citizens only at ruinous costs. There is also the feeling that the pursuit of specialization, on which higher and higher income and prestige usually depend, is sapping the professions' will and resources to serve the more ordinary needs of citizens. In sum, the public seems increasingly doubtful that the professions are living up to their part of the societal bargain, their historic commitment to stand ready to serve client and society in ways not always carefully calibrated to their own personal gain. Citizens also notice the minuscule number of professionals who are excluded from practice or otherwise disciplined each year by various professional and legal bodies, and suspect that professionals' first instinct is automatically to defend their beleaguered colleagues, rather than to protect the interests of their clients and of the public.

Internal problems also plague some of the major professions. One of the traditional marks of the professions is professional autonomy. The well-trained professional, engaged by a client, exercises his/her own best professional judgment about the best course of action to take to achieve the client's goal, and needs at the time of such judgment to consult no one other than the client about the choice made. Perhaps the most important element of this autonomy is the significant independence from lay judgment, i.e., from the judgment of any persons not equally trained in that profession. But as doctors begin to mirror the situation of most lawyers by becoming employees of large, often for-profit, organizations, such autonomy is often hedged about by the financial interests of the managed care agency. In such settings, many doctors no longer feel they can practice medicine as they think best, following only the needs of the patient and the dictates of their own expertise and commitment.

Some may consider law and medicine too remote from management to be helpful in understanding management's situation. But for most persons these two remain the paradigmatic professions. The fact that they also most conspicuously embody the advantages to which members of other occupations most often aspire when they seek professional standing is not coincidental.

There is a danger in suggesting, just as women are gaining access to some of the positions of privilege and power from which they have long been unjustly excluded, that we should reconsider the privilege and power that attaches to those positions. This suggestion might easily be seen as an attempt to keep women from having "their turn." Furthermore, this line of argument may seem to suggest that those who have been the victims of such exclusion should now become the agents of moral reform to redeem both the institutions which excluded them and the groups who unfairly monopolized those privileged positions. This last possibility involves an additional gender-based danger, for it may assume that just as women were once seen in the middle- and upper-class United States as the morally pure guardians of the sanctuary of the home, from which men went out to wrest a living from a morally ambiguous, even morally chaotic world, so now as these moral paragons move into the professions, they must work their magic of moral transformation there also, and in the process, quite possibly reduce the advantages that drew them to those positions. This is an unfair burden to put on women and is based on a poorly grounded assumption that women as such constitute the more moral part of the race and thus are peculiarly responsible for raising and maintaining the moral tone of our life together, whether in the home, the workplace, or the public square. The dangerous other side of this assumption, of course, is that it may seem to grant men license to conduct themselves in morally less demanding ways since they are constitutionally less fit for taking the moral high road.

But if Christians are to live out the solidarity Andolsen rightly calls for, if we are to act out our concern for the well-being—spiritual and moral as well as material—of all those touched by the power structures of the contemporary professions and of business, whether those persons obviously subject to the demands of those structures or of those ostensibly controlling them, we must pursue these questions in spite of the risks of misunderstanding and misinterpretation. If we remember that the reason for this reconsideration of the role of the professions and of management is not simply that women are now entering these areas in larger numbers, but rather that, for various reasons, the professions and management are currently in transition, then we can significantly reduce those risks.

There are at least three interconnected gains possible through such reconsideration: improved understanding of the obstacles to the entry of women and minorities into the professions and management; renewed understanding of and commitment to the traditional moral dimensions of the professions; rethinking the societal/moral meaning of management.

Women have made considerable strides in entering the professions, but their movement toward the upper levels in the professions remains slow. There is here neither space nor time to cite all the reasons women and minorities have had only very restricted access to the professions and continue to find progress in them difficult. But even a cursory review of some of them will illuminate other important issues. Any persons taking a biblically informed view of this question will have to invoke the category of sin to explain many such obstacles. Probably the most frequent forms of sin involve the disproportionate self-interest of the groups that have traditionally held a virtual monopoly over such prized positions and are reluctant to share the privileges attached to them. The rationalization of such exclusion often involves the additional sins of prejudicial perceptions or stereotypes of the groups excluded, and the discriminatory policies growing out of those perceptions. We must identify these obstacles and root them out. But if these are to be steps toward God's *shalom*, of which Roels speaks, we must, even while acknowledging that some are perhaps more guilty of these failings than others, remain aware that we are all vulnerable to them, both as victims and as perpetrators. Otherwise, we are in danger of continuing the same patterns while simply changing the roles of the various players, resulting in the "same game, different names" syndrome.

We must also remember that not all the sins met here represent the failings of current occupants of the positions and systems that must be transformed. The sins of the fathers (and mothers) are indeed visited upon the children to the third and fourth generations (Exod. 20:5). Whether we call it "organizational sin" (Roels) or institutionalized sin, we continue to live with both the good and the ill that past generations have structured into our institutions, our patterns of conduct, and even our ways of thinking. But even here, while struggling to right such wrongs, we must resist a self-indulgent and judgmental self-righteousness. For what to us so clearly seem to be the structures of sin were in past times seen quite differently, perhaps with good reason, although this does not mean that we must today accept those reasons. We also meet in this struggle the moral ambiguity of the right deed done for the wrong reasons, or the wrong deed done for reasons that then seemed, or were in fact, right. Agree or not with such actions and/or the reasons for them, if we are, without rancor and self-righteousness, to move toward the *shalom* God wills for all of us, we must be able to see the failings of the past with the same charity we hope for from future generations when they consider our performance.

Once we have identified and hedged about sinful forces such as self-interest and discrimination at work, the focus often rightly turns to the issue of qualifications for the position sought. But this too is a complex issue which can create new openings for divisive self-interest and discrimination. The first question is whether stated or assumed requirements for specific functions, positions, or even professions do in fact reflect what is needed to do the job well, or whether they came to be treated as "requirements" because they were compatible with or even essential to a particular and limited understanding of the profession. Is a "strong pulpit presence," presumably including booming voice and appropriate physical bearing, essential to being a Protestant minister, or does its significance hinge on a particular and even questionable conception of the ministry, shaped for and by the males who have historically dominated it? Do some of our expectations about physicians' need for interpersonal skills, bedside manner and commanding presence rest on a paternalistic understanding of the physician-patient relationship, and a commander-troops understanding of the physician's relation to the rest of the medical staff? Do our assumptions about how managers should exercise power and control personnel and processes reflect certain gender-based and gender-biased assumptions about what management is and how it should be executed?

Even after we have agreed on *bona fide* qualifications, there are several questions yet to be asked: have we stated them and devised tests for them in gender-neutral terms? Do we really know how to test whether and to what extent a specific applicant possesses the required trait or ability? If the applicant falls short, can we tell whether it is because of personal inadequacies, or because of societal commissions (imposed disabilities) or omissions (e.g., failure to educate in a gender- or ethnically neutral fashion)? Thus even a shift to *bona fide* qualifications for admission, retention, and advancement is no guarantee that we have removed all the obstacles to fair and equitable treatment.

As we consider qualifications—what it takes to be a competent or even exemplary member of a given profession—we are pressed to consider what the larger purpose or goal of that profession is. But this question about any specific profession must be answered within the larger question of why the professions, as a distinctive group of occupations, exist at all, why society gave birth to and now retains and sustains the professions.[6]

To consider the function, and therefore the justification of the professions, we need to come to some general agreement on just what distinguishes the professions from other occupations. While there seems to be widespread agreement on some of the following traits, even in this culture there is no unanimity about their being essential to the professions. Any effort at such a consensus is complicated by the facts that "professional associations" now cover all sorts of occupations and "unprofessional behavior" can be applied to virtually anyone in the workplace. I will, nevertheless, try to show why we should carefully weigh these distinctive traits of the professions, along with their historical standing and their current implications, before we abandon them. However, one danger of making the following four traits central to the professions is that we may end with a rather dated and exclusive, even elitist, model of the professions. The reader will have to judge whether these risks are balanced by the benefits of the following understanding of the professions.

Specialized Knowledge

For many people the most basic requirement of being a professional is that one be a member of a group that collectively and individually possesses specialized knowledge and skills not possessed by the public at large. Currently for groups incontestably holding full professional standing, such knowledge and skills are attained in a formal course of study publicly recognized as essential to one's being a professional of a given type. Traditionally—and to a large degree, currently—such specialized knowledge includes an understanding of the theory on which the profession's practice is based. This understanding of the theory behind the practice has sometimes been seen as distinguishing professionals from technicians.

Distinctive Goal

However, not just any body of specialized skills and knowledge will serve as the foundation for a profession. The knowledge and skills of the professional are seen as crucial tools for attaining and/or retaining a distinctive sort of goal. The orientation of the profession, its practice and therefore of its skills and knowledge toward this special sort of goal is the second traditional trait of the professions. While these distinctively professional goals can be characterized only with difficulty, two factors seem to be essential. First, the goals which we pursue with the assistance of professionals are not simply specific goods and services, although these latter may be some of the professionals' tools. They are, rather, states of being or states of affairs; thus they are most often intangible or even abstract. We seek health and healing from doctors, justice from lawyers, spiritual health or faith from clergy, knowledge from professors. Furthermore, how these are to be attained is often not clear to the layperson. Thus I go to the professional not with a list of specific goods and services I require, but with a request for assistance in attaining a goal that eludes me, and with the expectation that the professional will know how best to attain it and will help me do so.

Second, this condition or state of affairs for the attaining of which I seek professional assistance is one that I, presumably the professional, and a broad societal consensus see as being quite valuable because it is crucial to a fully and truly humane life, it is part of the truly good life for the individual client and for the society itself. I do not go to the professional for food and drink. These are ordinary and recurring needs the meeting of which I should either have mastered myself or know how to accomplish in the marketplace.

The distinctive nature and importance of the state I seek with the professional's help gives my relation to the professional a significant moral dimension. This dimension is heightened by the fact that in order to be helped I often must not only expose my need to the professional, but must take other steps which make me even more vulnerable—confessing my sins to the priest, exposing my inner life to the psychiatrist, submitting my body to the physician for surgery or other dangerous and invasive practices, or telling my lawyer what *really* happened. Thus I put the professional in a position to do significant harm to me and my interests through neglect, incompetence, or malice. Because I entrust her or him with such weighty matters, I need to be able to trust the professional in ways and to an extent not called for in other economic transactions.[7]

Self-Regulation

A third characteristic of the professions and of professionals is a level of autonomy not shared by many nonprofessional occupational groups. This autonomy or self-governance is enjoyed by the various professions in varying degrees and forms. In any given instance, it may include the profession's virtual control over the standards and procedures for admitting new members; over the preparation of aspiring members; over the investigation, judging, and disciplining of purportedly errant members; and over the standards of professional practice. In the case of the individual professional, such autonomy often means the right to make one's own decision about the path to be followed, and the methods to be used in assisting the client without being subject to assessment by any nonprofessional, or even, at the time of decision, by other members of one's own profession. Such insulation from lay assessment is never absolute. The doctor accused of negligently contributing to the death of a patient will have to answer to civil or criminal as well as to professional authorities. Nevertheless, the professions have traditionally enjoyed and continue to aspire to an autonomy in these matters which far exceeds that of virtually all nonprofessionals. It is perhaps one of the most prized prerogatives of professional standing.

Professionals can make a persuasive case that such autonomy is best not only for themselves, but for their clients and the society—after all, should lay persons, lacking the professionals' specialized skills and knowledge, control the education and admission of new members, the rules of practice, the assessment of professional performance? But it is still a costly and possibly risky thing for society to grant the professions such autonomy. Among other things, it grants the profession a virtual, or sometimes an actual monopoly, usually enforced by societally supported licensure laws, over certain crucial and highly valued areas of the society's and the client's life. This often means that: the usual market dynamics will not prevent overcharging; in terms of discipline and self-regulation, the in-group may prefer its own interests to those of client and society; and a profession may, by indifference or through fear of losing elements of its role, neglect or even obstruct new ways clients may achieve their goals.

Moral Commitment

This potential conflict of interests between the profession and the larger society, both individually (with regard to clients) and collectively, makes it a risky thing to put such power in the hands of a single self-regulating and self-perpetuating group. The only reason this granting by society of such autonomy to the professions has made any sense at all is because of the fourth major trait of the professions.

The professions have historically claimed, and through their various oaths, codes of conduct, principles of ethics, and disciplinary procedures often continue to claim to have, in the area of their professional expertise, a moral commitment to the interests of their clients and ultimately to the society not calibrated to their own self-interests, a moral commitment we normally do not expect of other economic agents. This atypical moral commitment professed by the profession then becomes the public's and the client's surety against the abuse of the powers, including the various forms of autonomy, that society has granted to the professions.

One way to see the relation between the traditional professions and the larger society as mediated through these four traits is in terms of the once emphatically, but now for many only dimly religious or theological terms of "covenant," and of "calling" or "vocation." Seen from this perspective, the central element in being a professional is the atypical moral commitment of the professional to assist individual clients and the society in the pursuit of the goals which are the focus of professional expertise. The fact that this readiness to serve has typically not been seen as being carefully calibrated to the professional's own self-interest gives rise to the open-endedness rightly associated with covenants as seen in Yahweh's dealing with ancient Israel at Sinai and in the bride and groom's brave commitment to each other "in sickness and in health, for better or for worse." This virtually unconditional commitment of the parties to each other binds them together in spite of, or perhaps because of, the unknown future they now share. Such a relation fits best where this sort of commitment to one's fellows and to the community is reflected in other segments of the society and is a significant part of a shared understanding of what it means to be a member of a community.

The fact that such commitment extends beyond what "common sense" and the immediate self-interest of the professional would normally dictate means that some larger, perhaps even transcendent ground must underlie such a commitment. For Jews and Christians such relations among persons make sense because they are called into them by the God who calls all persons into a similar relation with God, and therefore whose love and concern includes all parties to such a relationship. In its rightly theological meaning, a calling is not simply a career by which one pulls one's own weight and supports oneself and one's dependents. It is a view of one's relation to a larger reality, to one's community, even to the whole human community, which includes a commitment to serve the well-being, the common good, of that community.

The contemporary fading of such a sense of covenanted community, and of a caller who can and does call us into such a community creates an opening for another view of the profession/professional-society relation more consonant with the currently rampant individualism. This view casts the relation more in terms of a kind of contract or tradeoff between society and the professions. Two, possibly three, of the four traits now represent the professionals' costs: they will have to invest time, energy, and money in acquiring the requisite specialized knowledge and skills; and when taken seriously, the distinctive nature of the goal sought for client and/or society in professional activity, combined with the atypical moral commitment, set limits to the professionals' pursuit of their own self-interest. In part to balance these "costs" to the profession and the professional, the society grants them the privilege of autonomy. Currently on the benefits side, most professions also enjoy status and income significantly higher than those of the population at large. But this results from various internal and external social, political, and economic factors and should not be treated as essential marks of a profession.

Unfortunately the evolution does not stop here. As fewer and fewer factors effectively challenge the me-first individualism of our time, and the dominant shared wisdom of the time counsels us to take care of ourselves and our own since no one else will, and as professionals increasingly see themselves as exclusive proprietors of their skills and knowledge, both established and aspiring professions understandably focus on the benefit side and neglect the cost side of their bargain with society, eroding the professions' traditional moral role. If unchecked, this reshaping of the professionals' role should at some point prompt society to resurrect the covenanted community, or, if that is too big a challenge for our time, at least to renegotiate and enforce the contract.

How does this view of the professions relate to Roels's discussion of men and women in management? It will be recalled that in the context of two developments—the increasing numbers of women in the workplace, especially in management; and the emergence and continuing evolution of management as a profession—Roels raises three key concerns which she believes Christians should consider in light of their faith. These are: how Christians should understand their work—primarily in relation to God and to the rest of their lives (calling); and two major areas of responsibility for Christians in management (leadership and culture [-building]).

The most direct link between this discussion of the professions and Roels's three major concerns is through her assumption that management is increasingly becoming a profession. The questions of whether mine is an adequate understanding of the professions and, if so, whether management displays or can display the four traits I discuss, might be of interest only to students of the professions and/or of management, if it were not for the second, more pervasive link between the two discussions. This link arises from the fact that, as is suggested by its place in her essay, Roels's most fundamental point is about how we understand our work, specifically about the importance of seeing our work as part of, but not as the entirety of our vocation. It is largely from her position on how we should see our work that the rest of her discussion springs.

The significance of this broader connection can perhaps best be seen through a discussion of the following assertions. Much of what Roels wishes to accomplish with the concept of Christian vocation can be and historically has been done in this culture with the concept of the professions. If the important points she makes are to be taken seriously beyond the Christian community—an increasingly important issue as we move into a global economy and, it is to be hoped, a global community—we will need a more inclusive vehicle than Christian vocation to carry them, for while we believe the one God calls Christian and non-Christian alike, this is probably not the language most conducive to discussion of these matters across confessional lines. While in some ways "profession" as traditionally understood might serve as such a vehicle, casting management in the mold of the traditional professions may be more difficult than Roels realizes.

Put most briefly, Roels's position on vocation or calling is that Christians must see their employment, their paid work, not just in relation to their own needs and aspirations and those of their dependents, but in relation to God and God's intentions for the world. Presumably one important theological point undergirding this position is that the sovereignty of the God whom Christians worship encompasses every aspect of our lives. The one God is Lord not only of religious and personal or family matters, but of the cultural, the scientific, the political, and the economic dimensions of God's one world. Thus the larger point is that every part of our lives must be seen in light of what God intends for the world. If then the God we worship intends well for God's world and all of God's people, intends the human family to flourish, intends for them, in Roels's properly biblical language, *shalom*, then we must see to it not only that no aspects of our lives work against that *shalom*, but that they actually contribute to it. Thus she suggests that Christians must help all people to see their work as vocation or calling so that all together can ask which goods and services, even which professions or occupations, contribute to the well-being of the human family, and which do not. This is a very different and potentially much more disruptive question than is the currently dominant one about which goods and services will survive in the market place, or which occupations will guarantee me high income, prestige, and job security.

Of course Roels's question will introduce further difficult, Hydra-headed questions which will multiply faster than we can answer them: Who defines *shalom*? Who gets to say what contributes to *shalom* and what does not? By what authority? Using what criteria? Must all goods and services contribute to *shalom*, or must they just not be destructive of it? What if some don't share our idea of *shalom* (preferring, perhaps, liberation, or illumination, or release, or Nirvana)? Must they comply with the same restrictions? What sorts of enforcement are appropriate? But the difficulty of these questions must not deter us from struggling with them, lest the public discussion of such matters be deprived of the Christian voice.

These questions become simultaneously more important and more complex as we consider a future of limited, dramatically shrinking resources in relation to the needs of the growing human family. In such a situation we must be concerned not only with products that are destructive of *shalom* and of human flourishing, but with products that consume limited resources while making no positive contribution to the increasingly desperate needs of the world. Such issues begin to show us just how transforming Roels's "world-transforming faith" might be.

While Roels would have Christians enrich their concept of work and profession by seeing them as a calling, she also strongly cautions against reducing our calling, or our personal identity, to our work. Theologically speaking, the same sovereignty of God which tells us that we cannot place our economic activity outside the realm of God's intentions for the world also tells us that work cannot become an idol, a mini-god which eliminates all the other dimensions of our calling and thus become the sole definer of who we are. Roels sees this last possibility as one of the traps many moderns, perhaps especially professionals, have fallen into and which is to be avoided by Christians. Roels is aware that these two parts of her position may create some tension for Christians, for she simultaneously elevates work as part of our calling, but limits it as only *part* of our calling. The fact, as she sees it, that the work of management is increasingly professional work tends to reinforce the work-elevating part of her proposal for the various reasons she cites, and so may aggravate the temptation to let work become our entire calling, our entire identity.

But even if the professional work of management is only *part* of our calling, it *is* part of our *calling*. Two responsibilities of management that are transformed by this insight are leadership and culture building. In the former, the leader must still lead. But such leadership must be exercised in ways that encourage, even nurture, the dignity, rights, contributions, and growth—the *shalom*—of all affected by that leadership. Thus leadership cannot be reduced to the simple attainment of certain goals. It also has to do with how one gets there. As Roels puts it: "The purpose for the administrative gift in conjunction with all other gifts is building up the human community in service to God and each other."

Management's culture-building responsibilities are also affected when Christians see management as part of their calling. The kind of culture to be built now is not determined solely by "bottom line" considerations such as productivity, efficiency, and profitability. The culture to be developed is to be shaped also by concern for all affected parties as persons and as members of the community, not simply as part of the productive process. Roels's concern about women's situation in the workplace means that one pervasive concern in the discussion of leadership and culture is that women be treated appropriately, both as persons aspiring to roles as leaders and culture builders, and as persons subject to the leadership and culture building of others.

This brings us to my four convictions, which are both extensions of and friendly amendments to Roels's position. First, I believe that much of what Roels wishes to accomplish with the concept of Christian vocation can be and historically has been done in Western cultures with the concept of the professions. Roels seems to think that one of the major changes that her proposal about how we see

111

work would make is that such work would now be oriented toward service to others and to the communities we all inhabit. In other words, the horizon or the perspectives from which our performance is assessed would be enlarged from questions of how well is this position serving me and the corporation, to how well is it serving the communities of which we are all ultimately a part.

As I have defined the professions, they too have traditionally pushed the professional to look beyond self-interests to the interests of the client, and ultimately to those of the larger society. Just as a lawyer, even while defending her client, is still an officer of the court, and is still held responsible for the integrity of the court system as one of society's major tools for establishing and defending justice, so all the traditional professionals were on some level agents of the society in its pursuit of the goals peculiar to that profession, even while they labored on behalf of specific clients. It is precisely this dual loyalty that continues to generate some of the most perplexing problems for the traditional professions. This orientation, even obligation, to the larger society was rooted to a large degree in the fact that the goal sought by both the professional and client was one that the society itself highly prized for its members and for itself as a whole. The professions as we know them are not created in private by small, exclusive groups of like-minded persons. They were and are societal creations through and through. Thus the professional's pursuit of health or justice or knowledge for the client is simultaneously part of society's pursuit of those same goals for itself and all its members. Interestingly, Roels brings in this service orientation only in her discussion of vocation or calling, and not in conjunction with the professions. Thus her essay may reflect the diminishment of this service orientation, from which the professions have been suffering for some time.

Of course the concept of management as a profession does not tie management to God, and certainly not in any specific ways to the biblical God of whom Roels speaks. In the West, the religious roots of the professions, both as a concept (note the two currently dominant ordinary uses of "profession"—as a proclaiming of one's faith and as a distinctive set of occupations) and as having derived at least in part from the clergy (law, teaching, medicine) have long since faded. But, as the following paragraphs suggest, this religious "failure" of the concept of the professions may not be a disadvantage. On the other hand, the concept of the professions may help specify the direction and nature of the service to be rendered with more precision than do the related ideas of calling and *shalom*. Clients and potential clients seeking the aid of contemporary professionals usually know quite clearly the sorts of services they seek and the goals at which those services aim. One question about management as a profession, to be discussed below, is whether it can specify such a distinctive professional goal for itself as can law, medicine, or the ministry.

My second conviction is that if the important points Roels makes are to get any hearing beyond the Christian community, they will need a vehicle more inclusive than Christian vocation to carry them. Even though we write here as Christians to a largely Christian audience, I believe we must continue to struggle to get our theology and our articulation of it broad enough to include the entire globe of which we profess our God to be Lord. If God continues to relate to the earth's peoples without first making them Jews or Christians, we should honor the inclusiveness of God's care by struggling for a similar inclusiveness in our understanding of ourselves, our fellows, and our God. This is not to betray our own heritage. It is simply to acknowledge the limits of our language and concepts, of our understanding and imagination. Thus when Roels writes that "the root of a person's working identity should be each human's relationship to the living God . . . the One who said, 'Let us make humankind in our image, according to our likeness,'" it may seem to many readers that all of "non biblical" humanity is left out of the discussion. Much of what she wishes to convey here can be stated in a more inclusive way, to indicate that our identity as humans must be rooted in some foundation broad enough and deep enough to support, and to help us understand and cope with, all aspects of our lives and of our world. Gender and work, the two foundations Roels rightly rejects, are clearly inadequate to this task. Christians will no doubt find such a foundation in the Living God of whom Roels speaks. But that is not to say others cannot find other foundations, or perhaps the same foundation differently articulated.

Having argued for "the professions" as one possible candidate for that more inclusive vehicle to carry some of Roels's ideas beyond Christian audiences, I must now ask if casting management in the mold of the traditional professions may not be more difficult than Roels indicates. Roels's argument for management having become a profession hinges largely on the change in the education of managers

113

sometime after the middle of this century. Preparation for a career in management went from "how to do" instruction to "how to think" instruction, taking the social sciences as a major part of its theoretical base. This, of course, relates directly to the issue of the professions' specialized skills and knowledge. But this concerns only the *competence* part of being a professional. We need to look at management also in terms of the *commitment* dimensions of the professions, a dimension more evident in the covenantal than in the contractual construal of the profession/society relationship.

For a number of reasons, I believe that management will have difficulty measuring up to the model of the traditional professions I have suggested. I will list several of these reasons simply to put them on record, but will not treat them at length since they are not immediately involved in the major difficulty I will cite.

Traditional professions have specific and identifiable clients, even though they may, as in the cases of professors and the clergy, be corporate or collective as well as individual. Who are the manager's clients and for what do they seek the manager's professional assistance? The exercise of professional skills by the traditional professionals most often has a *direct* and *immediate* impact on their clients. The impact of managers on clients, such as company owners and boards of directors, occurs only through the intermediate agency of numerous other persons (other levels of management, workers, perhaps consumers themselves) and of complex processes over which they have only indirect control. Can the categories of professional responsibility and direct accountability be applied in such situations?

The issue of the autonomy of a profession as a whole and of the individual practitioner raises multiple problems here. Autonomy of the profession usually means considerable influence on, if not actual control of, formal preparation for admission to the profession; the processes of examination and licensure by which one becomes a member of the profession; and of the disciplining of errant members. But in management, records of past performance will almost certainly remain better admission tickets than M.B.A or even Ph.D. degrees. Given the diversity of the settings in which they operate, the sophistication of what they actually do, and the kinds of training and experience that they have, are managers as a group likely to want to, and even if so, likely to find it possible to create a professional organization to take on these tasks? Is it likely that General Motors will be denied the right to hire Maria Rodriquez as CEO because she is not a licensed manager and does not even have an M.B.A., just as a hospital cannot hire a non-M.D. as head surgeon? And how much autonomy can we envision for a manager who, even if she sits at the top of the managerial pyramid, is still directly subject to the will and whimsy of the board of directors, who may or may not be as experienced and knowledgeable about management as she, and in a still more complex way is subject to the will of investors working in part through the often indecipherable gyrations of the stock market?

But, given the nature of our concerns here, the most important questions about management being a profession in the fullest traditional sense arise in relation to the moral or *commitment* dimensions of the professions, dimensions I have tied most closely to the traits of having a distinctive goal of widely recognized fundamental value to client and society toward which the professional helps the client, and of having an atypical moral commitment in the area of professional expertise to the interests of the client, even, on occasion, at the expense of the professional's own self-interest. Concerning the first, what distinctive professional goal do the professional manager and her client(s) aim at together? Assume that Roels's and my similar suggestions are accepted, and we see the goal of management as contributing to the *shalom* of the human family by helping generate goods and services that sustain and enhance human life in community, which help humankind flourish. Are managers currently, or in any foreseeable future, likely to be the persons who know best the meaning of such goals and how to achieve them? This clearly would require a thorough-going revolution in what we mean by management, in how we prepare persons for a career in management, and in how we assess their performance. This is not to say that managers currently are less committed to the well-being of the human race than are the rest of us. It is simply to be realistic about what we currently mean by management and the role it currently plays in society.

But the most difficult obstacle to management's becoming a profession in the fullest moral sense is yet to be treated. Clearly, in speaking of management here, Roels and I have in mind primarily the management of for-profit business enterprises in the sort of mixed capitalist economy now found in the United States. That economy still runs, or at least is assumed by most to run, primarily on the fuel of the competing self-interests of all its participants. Although often denied by top-level management in more formal, ceremonial settings, many still seem persuaded by Adam Smith's argument that this is not only an inescapable natural fact, but that it is also a good thing for individuals and society because without intending it, we are likely to produce more societal good through the pursuit of our own self-interest than we are likely to produce in any other way. If this understanding of our market economy is not only widespread but is generally endorsed, then a fundamental reorientation is necessary if professional managers pursuing the goals of which Roels and I speak are to hold responsible positions in contemporary business. Such a revolution seems unlikely in the extreme. Thus the emergence and survival of a profession of management in the fullest sense, including the moral sense, seems to me equally unlikely. Again, my pessimism about the possibility of such transformations in our economic system and the managers who run it does not imply any particular moral failure or deficiency in terms of the system itself, nor of those who participate in it. Such "pessimism" is simply a realistic recognition that the system that has developed in this and similar settings to motivate and reward economic activity seems in fundamental ways to be at odds with Roels's vision.

Even if Christian managers were to take seriously Roels's arguments about management as a calling, what is the likelihood of their having a significant impact on the current system? The answer to that question is important because of what it would tell us not only about the likely fate of such individual Christians, but also about the potential of the Christian community for transforming the world in this way. The conflict that I have suggested exists between the service orientation that Roels proposes for management and even for business itself, and the self-interest and profit orientation of a marketplace economy, is precisely the conflict that many health care professionals are feeling between their traditional orientation to the client's interests and the profit orientation of so many managed care organizations. Many practitioners, along with many observers of this change in health care, seem currently convinced that the market orientation is more likely to transform the professional orientation than vice versa.

Finally, while I believe the transformation of the economy and of management along the lines Roels hopes for is currently unlikely, I believe she is correct that the crucial element in such changes is the fundamental reorientation of such activity. Furthermore, I believe she has given an entirely defensible biblical answer to that question—that the economy and our own economic activity, like all the areas of our lives, must aim at the *shalom*, the flourishing of all of God's people. Were this to happen, management could then claim to be a profession in the fullest sense. But this would represent such a fundamental transformation of our world that the professional status of management would become a trivial issue.

With Roels, I long for the sort of reorientation of economic life she envisions, at least to the extent that I can imagine what it would be like. I agree that such a vision is well-rooted in the Hebrew and Christian Scriptures and in much of the thought and life that has sprung from them. But I have argued that seeing management as a profession or, better yet, seeing to it that management becomes a profession in the fullest sense, is not the way to effect those transformations. But the careful reader will note that this does not put me in direct conflict with Roels since she seems not to suggest that the full professionalization of management is the way to achieve this end. Why then suggest this possibility, only to reject it? I propose it, in part, because I believe the professions have in some crucial areas of our lives effected or at least worked toward an orientation similar to the one she proposes. I also raise the issue of management's becoming a profession because I believe that the professions have, in theory, and to some extent in practice, been an important way for society to set off certain crucial areas of our lives together, to protect them from being exploited by the potentially destructive motives that often characterize much of our economic lives. If this is true, then it is important to all of us that we protect the concept of the professions from being eviscerated to the point that it cannot protect such areas in this way. The most frequent form of weakening, especially as new occupations struggle to become professions, is permitting the moral dimensions of the professions to atrophy.

But there is a final reason for exploring this possibility of management as a profession bringing about such a reorientation. If management could become a profession in the sense laid out above, then it would be a major tool in reorienting not only management, but the economic system that managers manage. Much of that effectiveness would derive from the fact that the professions are, as noted above, societal creations through and through. Thus the emergence of management as a full-blown profession would presumably mean that the reorientation of management and of business was already well underway as a public enterprise. That would seem to augur better for the success of such a reorientation than does changing the way Christians in business, and perhaps the Christian communities from which they come, envision management and business.

In other words, we face here the question of how a Christian presence in the world, a Christian influence in changing the world, is to be made real. Are we, when possible, to enlist, and perhaps become dependent upon, the resources of the larger society, as would be the case if management could become a profession with an enlarged moral vision derived from or at least paralleling Roels's biblical sense of what economic activity ought to be about? But does this not also introduce the possibility that the Christian vision will be co-opted or subverted? Perhaps Roels, for these reasons, wisely keeps the Christian re-visioning of management and of economic activity separate from the emerging professionalization of management. Or is the Christian presence to be felt more through the vision, the convictions, and the resulting actions of believers, who must follow their callings whether or not the world comes along? Whether or not this is the reason Roels keeps calling and profession largely separate in her discussion, I believe she is correct in doing so. We are called first to be faithful Christians in the ways we see and intend the world. Only secondarily are we called to be effective in transforming it. The wisdom of serpents must keep us aware that in a fallen world, we may find ourselves intending it in directions it will not go. Christian managers following their calling as managers may find themselves defeated by an economic system that refuses to swear allegiance to the *shalom* of the human family. This raises one possibility that Roels does not consider, but on which we can not automatically foreclose if we are to be open to the realities of our fallen world and to the Spirit's prompting. This is that management in the economic system that currently dominates in this country may, in at least some instances, be one of those occupations that does not fit with our calling to work toward *shalom*. It may be that Christians are no more likely soon to be counted among the majority in how economic activity is understood and managed than they are to be counted among the majority of the world religiously.

Chapter 4

In Response

Shirley J. Roels

Both Barbara Andolsen and Paul Camenisch have added significantly to my exploration of gender issues in organizational life. I have learned from their considerate essays, and their ideas have added new questions and fresh perspectives on the matters that we are mapping. The three of us share similar concerns for gender-related justice and equity in society. Yet, with different configurations of knowledge and life experience, the nuances differ. In my response to them, I will comment on our similarities and differences.

Barbara Andolsen and I have much in common. Her theological touchstones of justice, solidarity, and social sin are compatible with my own for many reasons, including the fact that we are both trying to work with Christian ideas. Her explication of these concepts as the basis for evaluating the effects of gender on occupations is helpful. Biblical justice does require a never-ending commitment to the marginalized as well as their participation in decisions which affect their lives. Solidarity, defined as the emphasis on balancing individual freedom with common good, is woven throughout the Judeo-Christian Scriptures, and finds expression in all the great streams of the faith. Andolsen's explication of social sin as moral blindness and moral callousness also fits the description of sin Jesus accented; it, too, is biblical.

I share Andolsen's concern for distributive justice related to the structure of occupations. Among occupational classifications and within a given occupation, justice—understood as equitable access—should be a concern. Andolsen's evidence points to the fact that not only are we individual sinners in our gender relations at work, but we are also all caught in webs of broader, sometimes sin-laden, structural phenomena. These national occupational structures are, in turn, framed and sometimes reinforced by current global developments. This appears to be particularly true regarding the widening wage gaps between different occupations within the United States, a matter Paul Camenisch also identifies. The framework for valuing different types of jobs now depends more on both the increased demand (thus higher pay) for highly trained workers and managers and the increased supply of less trained labor, under conditions in which the global supply of those with little education and skill is vast and accessible. Worldwide, there are many men and women willing to work for wages that are less than 10 percent of the wages that the same jobs have traditionally commanded in North America. At the same time the demand for knowledge and expertise at senior managerial levels is not similarly spread across the globe. Thus, the compensation gaps between our occupations are being exacerbated (and are likely to continue for at least some time).

Who comprehends whether the net global effect is helpful or harmful? Jobs flow to men and women in less industrialized countries who previously had no income. Wages that are pitiful by our standards feed entire families elsewhere, and may even reflect an emerging broader solidarity, a wider common good. Yet simultaneously, the growing gap between the wages of different occupations in the United States further fractures the sense of middle-class nationhood that has served our democracy and our common identity. Andolsen rightly notes that these factors inhibit gender equity in the United States, particularly when we are oblivious to their effects on the differential valuing of occupations. I concur with her judgment that equitable access to quality education for both women and men is a key factor in the equitable use of their talents in the twenty-first century.

Andolsen also serves us well by extending the gender-related discussion specifically to women who are clerical and temporary workers, those pressured to care for both children and elderly family members, and to women of color in the labor force. I concur with her description of how technology has altered clerical and secretarial work while corresponding wage scales seem to have lagged behind. I share Andolsen's moral passion for those women who have not benefited from even the modest gains made by educated white women, and we both believe that all adults must keep commitments to the young and old within their families.

Yet while Barbara Andolsen and I share many Christian convictions and agree in many ways about what is happening in American society, our theology is not identical, our analyses have some dissimilarities, and our strategies for improvement vary. Let me explain.

First, Andolsen writes that "a Christian understanding of solidarity arises in part from an awareness that all human beings share a life affirming relationship with Sophia-Spirit." From this statement she proceeds to describe the nature of Sophia-Spirit and Divine Woman Wisdom, using Wisdom theology tied to a Hebraic spiritual tradition contemporaneous with Jesus. I do not invoke a gendered Holy Spirit, and this is not how I think we can best understand the locus or character of solidarity.

I concur with Andolsen that male imagery and concepts for God have been prevalent in most centuries since Christ's incarnation and that we need both male and female images for God so that as humans we can more fully understand God. It is, in fact, quite biblical to invoke female imagery for God. Isaiah describes the coming messenger of the Lord as one who will carry lambs in his bosom and gently lead those that are with young (Isa. 40:11). Jesus describes himself as one who would gladly be the mother hen gathering the brood of Jerusalem under her wing (Matt. 23:27). Such female similes, which enrich our understanding of God, should be explored.

Yet to talk of Sophia-Spirit as one of the persons of the Trinity seems to presuppose the very framework that I oppose, namely, the imposition of our limited human language on the God who is beyond gendered description. I am well aware that some feminists find great comfort in this idea, but I am not convinced that it does, or in the long run can, accomplish what it purports. Does not this approach run the risk of stressing opposing male/female characteristics for God instead of emphasizing God as the "I Am" who transcends sexual differences? For if God is beyond gender, then it is under, with, and in God that we can hope for both marital love relationships, where sexual distinctions make one kind of difference, and sexual complementarity in the workplace, where the distinction must be treated quite differently. Both are situations in which female and male mirror the image of God. Andolsen and I agree that women and men equally share the *imago Dei*. Yet one need not invoke a tradition that understood Jesus as the prophet of Sophia to reach that conclusion. That Jesus was a human male is not disputed, and given the culture of that time it might well have been odd for the Messiah to have been conceived otherwise. Yet treating the persons of the Trinity as sexed or gendered may properly be debated. In fact, some parts of the tradition may have become vulnerable to charges of sexism precisely for making that error. The *imago Dei* is not first of all a matter of gender, but of being in a full relationship to God and to others who are also made in that image.

Further, I believe it is better to see the Trinity as one God, comprised by persons beyond gender in community, and thus the basis for our unity as males and females, than to ascribe gendered character to different persons of the Trinity in ways that the Bible does not. Christian concern for women in the workplace, even the occupationally poor and marginalized, is not dependent on ascribing gender to persons of the Trinity. Thus, to me, the evidence for invoking the Sophia-Spirit is neither convincing nor necessary to the argument. On this point Andolsen and I differ.

Second, I believe some distinctions are critical in understanding distributional justice. Inequality of opportunity and access are social sins; but perhaps inequality of occupational results should not be similarly classified. Andolsen's statistics on sex-related distributions within professional and managerial jobs are accurate, as are her descriptions of how sex, race, and class intersect in occupational influence and options. Yet we must be careful.

Skewed outcome statistics appropriately raise red flags of investigation; but we cannot assume that all statistical differences within an occupation or between occupations are the inherent results of current discrimination. Instead, some differences reflect the slow process of social change at some levels, especially at the senior organizational level, and rapid processes of social change at other levels—such as the movement of masses of women into the workforce in the course of a generation. Senior positions are tied to decades of learning and experience, and to patterns of socialization, which most women born before 1950 did not factor into their lives. Thus, it takes considerably more time to create greater equity at senior levels that at lower levels, although in some situations impatience properly aids justice. In addition, the nondiscriminatory job access to which we committed ourselves in the 1960s and 1970s has been greatly complicated. Occupational reframing, tied to higher educational requirements, changing technology, and globalization in the 1980s and 1990s, has made this struggle more complex than we earlier imagined. Given these other factors, inequality of results will continue to induce anger and hostility, unless we disaggregate its complicated underlying causes and work on them one by one. We must therefore be very careful in our analysis to attend to the various factors that deny opportunity or access instead of focusing too much on current occupational statistics.

In a similar vein, while I believe that the sins of the past continue to influence present paths, I am not convinced that assigning current blame for historical discrimination, which some of the authors cited by Andolsen seem to do, is a practical tactic. In my experience, guilt does not motivate changed behavior. Thus, to hang the label of sexism or racism on an organization because of choices over which current individuals may have had little influence is not usually helpful. A more effective motivator is to provide current decision makers with a better vision of how things are supposed to be and then analyze the gap between the ideal and the current situation. This is a matter of practical strategy. However, too frequently, when the focus is principally on the assignment of blame, the acknowledgment that "We're sorry about the past" becomes the last step, not the first step, in a process. In fact, the acknowledgment of guilt has not always led to improvement, nor to actions that allow all to flourish.

Finally, my recommended strategies for progress are somewhat different than Andolsen's. I make finer distinctions in the forces that are operative in the behavior of a given labor market. While some labor economists may argue that there are several labor markets, as does Andolsen, others suggest hundreds and perhaps thousands of labor markets. For example, the market and related salaries for women clerical workers will depend on a multitude of factors in a given area: regional economic strength; demand for clerical workers in the region's industries; the area's quality of education and advanced training; the social and religious culture, which influences the desire for paid labor; the values of businesses; the range of competing opportunities; the costs and accessibility of transportation and of care for children and the elderly; the probability of outsourcing this work to other countries; and so on. The configuration and relative strength of these factors may vary and thus create labor market effects that are considerably different from region to region, industry to industry, technology to technology, and subculture to subculture.

The same range of factors influences demand and supply for part-time and contingent workers. I agree with Andolsen that, given the globalization of certain job fields, we cannot reverse employer demand for more flexibility in labor costs. For a given employer, if he or she does not control labor costs carefully, the results can be devastating in a competitive global economy. Higher product price, lower market share, lower net margins, unstable stakeholder value, bankruptcy, or vulnerability as a takeover target may all result from uncontrolled labor costs. For some employers in globalizing industries such as textiles and clothing, the choice has been between organizational survival with fewer permanent jobs and the collapse of the firm without such reductions in employment.

Thus, while I share Andolsen's concern for the plight of such workers and believe we should develop more sound national data about their situations, I am not prone to suggest either comprehensive federal solutions to wage inequities or formal public strategies to shrink the contingent workforce. Instead, I recommend decentralized regional solutions in which the partners must be businesses, local and state governments, churches, employer and employee associations. In particular I challenge employers to hire excellent human resource managers and allow them to construct creative jobs, reconfigure wage scales when necessary, identify paths to develop employee potential, advocate diversity, and become champions of equity. Human resource managers are some of the people best positioned to create a different future for those who need satisfying work, decent compensation, and some sense of personal stability. I also challenge those who manage staffing agencies for temporary workers to consider their responsibilities for providing not only short-term wages but long-term security in health coverage and retirement provisions for those in their care. Just because an employee is short term at a given company does not mean that no one should take responsibility for that employee's long-term needs and work-related goals; and the "temp-supplier" who develops ways to do this fairly and efficiently is likely to be at the cutting edge of that growing industry.

In regard to a related matter, I do not share Andolsen's opinion that unions can at this time be a strong vehicle for women pursuing occupational justice. I am not inherently opposed to unions. They have served and continue to serve some employee groups well when employees must have a collective voice to counterbalance the power of flawed employers. In the past, unions have contributed significantly to improvements in working conditions, decent compensation, and protection for employees. However, even if North American women would join unions in greater numbers, the field on which

124

unions and management play their game has changed. The field is no longer North American. It is far bigger than even the matured industrial world. It is truly a global field; and on this global field the international players do not play by the union/management rules of North America. The power of unions in many sectors has thus been strongly curtailed. We cannot reverse the globalization of the labor supply for many types of jobs; and, even where possible, it will take several decades before the labor movement gains any strength in many worldwide sources for workers. Thus, I resist the recommendation that women jump on the union bandwagon as a strategy for improving their job situations. Such energy should be channeled elsewhere.

Instead, I believe that the best hope for balancing the power of employers is the knowledge and skill that employees bring to their work. I agree with Andolsen that education can provide many more avenues of opportunity and support freer choice for employees. Knowledgable skillful women dissatisfied with their employers can quit because they will have opportunities with other employers or may begin their own organizations. Thus, strategically, access to educational opportunities for women is critical. I believe this will be a more effective avenue to independence and voice than unions can practically be in the next couple of decades.

Paul Camenisch takes the discussion in a quite different direction but certainly adds substantially to the conversation about the nature of management. We appear to agree substantially about issues of gender in organizational life. I appreciate Camenisch's comments about paths to gender equity as well as his sensitive suggestion that women be asked to carry only their fair share of moral guardianship. His ideas provide insight, and we agree on them. Thus, I will not comment further about his helpful additions to the discussion of gender. Instead, I will focus on his reflections about vocational theology and on his reservations about management as a profession.

I have no difficulty granting Camenisch's point that a theology of calling has inherent limits in reaching beyond those who explore Christian frames of thought and life. That may be so. However, I presumed that this volume was primarily addressed to those who wish to explore a Christian frame of reference. Obviously when one connects with those who operate in different faith frameworks the language of the discussion must change; and I agree with Camenisch that it is important to interact regularly with populations whose frame of reference is not Christian. In that regard Camenisch's suggestion that we consider the concept of "profession" as the bridge between differing world views is helpful and certainly merits further discussion.

Yet, we may need to inquire, as we enter the global conversation on these matters, whether certain aspects of Christian theology are generally valid and critical for humankind to sustain spiritual and moral meaning. If "profession," for example, becomes understood simply as "expert-for-hire," what could restore loyalty to the four qualities that Camenisch identifies? I think it remains an open question as to whether one can grasp the fuller significance of "profession" without a sense of both "vocation" and "covenant"; and I do not think that the meanings of these terms are too esoteric to be understood, embraced, or adapted by others as they "professionalize," and seek to do so with moral integrity.

That leads to my second area of comment, whether management should be considered as a profession. Camenisch argues that professions are characterized by several features that management inherently lacks. He argues that management may involve specialized knowledge or skill, yet it cannot be a profession because it does not have, and perhaps cannot have, direct client responsibilities separate from self-interest; it is not self-regulating or autonomous; and it cannot frame moral commitment to the common good as can the traditional professions. Our opinions differ both on what is and what can be.

First, I question whether Camenisch's view of the traditional professions is indeed the state in which they find themselves in the late twentieth century. Not all professionals have direct and dramatic client impact as these professions have become more internally differentiated. The type and level of impact varies dramatically within the various professions. Working lawyers will tell you that much litigation and paperwork seems far removed from direct client impact. Are clergy really all that self-regulating, even if traditional ecclesiastical frames of accountability have, for many of them, given way to nondenominational megachurches? Are physicians really that autonomous, given the advent of health maintenance organizations and group medical practices? Indeed, at another level, are we sure that the traditional professions today operate with a higher level of concern for the common good than those in professional-level occupations which have emerged in the past two centuries?

I sense that Camenisch maintains a somewhat romantic view of the traditional professions which does not honor the variety among them, or their locus in the late twentieth century. It is not all that easy for any occupational group to be fully professional at this juncture in history. Thus, to suggest that management cannot qualify seems to deny the contemporary struggles of other professions on these same issues.

Second, I do believe that one can legitimately argue that management can and does have many features of the other professions. Many managers do, indeed, have direct relationships to people's state of being, to their souls. Granted, not all goods and services have that effect on customers, but some may. For several decades now, we have had extended discussions about the fact that the clients of a manager are the employees and other stakeholders of an organization. These souls are affected by managers. Managers frame the purposes for work. Managers hire, develop, and promote people. Managers create environments of dignity or the lack thereof. Even more, management makes possible, under modern conditions, the creation of wealth—which is indispensable for both the common-wealth and the professions. Where their specialized skills are not available or are underdeveloped, poverty attends the human condition even more dramatically than it does where they are present. These are matters of our state of being.

It is true that management is not completely self-governing. However, managers are expected to exercise a significant amount of independent judgment every day in their organizations. They are responsible for the end results; yet they frequently have significant independence in how they achieve them. Is there really less autonomy here than in other professions, particularly when managers function across the globe and outside the constraints of tighter local communities and North American law?

Some self-regulation does occur in the managerial community. Accountants have ethical codes and standards for their work. Purchasing managers have codes of conduct that are shared in their network. Human resource managers aspire to honor the standards laid out by their professional organizations. Thus, there are some elements of professional self-regulation within the managerial community. There should be more; and further, theologically informed reflections about the moral nature of the managerial enterprise are likely to generate more such codes and professional standards. I see no reason to dismiss the prospect of self-regulation beforehand, especially since several such features already exist in these areas, as well as in "professional fields" such as engineering or architecture, which Camenisch does not discuss.

Finally, I believe that moral commitment which enhances the common good of society is possible in a global market economy. These are not inherently opposed at every turn. Granted, there will be compromises, and times when the nature of the competitive economic frame will not allow managers to perfectly balance individualized interests and the common good. However, that is different from ruling out the possibility of managers having the moral commitments of a professional. Any profession struggles to balance individual and societal interest. The struggle is not unique to management, but the challenge can be and ought to be part of management.

In the end, though, does the classification of management as a profession make the critical difference? I doubt it. It matters far less how an occupation is classified than what one does with one's occupation and how well that occupation intersects with one's holistic sense of calling. If those who have the talent for management reject the possibility that it can be part of a Christian calling, where would that leave society, or managers trying to be responsible? I fear the results if we simply give up on the quest for a theologically informed vision for organizational personnel who affect meaning, value, and the common good.

Thus, I prefer that we continue the struggle. Our Christian ideal is to transform this redeemed world so that each woman and man can be whom God intended, serving in this world as each is called. This is our responsibility as God's creatures. Yet we are the not the Creator, but creatures with limits on our time, talent, energy, vision and goodwill. Alas, we are mortal and sinful men and women. We will struggle. Yet I believe that our faithfulness will work for good. Thanks be to God that the final outcome rests in the hands of the One who is greater and wiser than us all.

Notes

Notes to Chapter 1

1. For a recent discussion which critiques the use of social science data in gender-related analysis, see Christina Hoff Sommers, *Who Stole Feminism?* (New York: Simon and Schuster, 1994).

2. These two reports were independently published in the same year but reached similar conclusions about business education. See Robert A. Gordon and James E. Howell, *Higher Education for Business* (New York: Columbia University Press, 1959), and Frank Cook Pierson, *The Education of American Businessmen* (New York: McGraw Hill, 1959).

3. Francis X. Sutton, Seymour E. Harris, Carl Kaysen, and James Tobin, *The American Business Creed* (New York: Schocken Books, 1956), 271ff.

4. William H. Whyte, Jr., *The Organization Man* (New York: Simon and Schuster, 1956).

5. Betty Friedan, *The Feminine Mystique* (New York: W. W Norton, 1963).

6. Margaret Hennig and Anne Jardim, *The Managerial Woman* (New York: Pocket Books, 1976).

7. Rosabeth Moss Kanter, *Men and Women of the Corporation* (New York: Basic Books, 1977).

8. Lewis Carroll, *Alice's Adventures in Wonderland* (New York: Signet Classics, 1960), 62.

9. Phyllis Trible, *God and the Rhetoric of Sexuality* (Philadelphia: Fortress Press, 1978), chapter 1.

10. Ibid., chapter 4.

11. Mary Stewart Van Leeuwen, ed., *After Eden* (Grand Rapids: Wm. B. Eerdmans Publishing Co., 1993), 170.

12. For further descriptions about concepts of vocation during the monastic era, see writings by Benedict and David Landes in the anthology, *On Moral Business: Classical and Contemporary Resources for Ethics in Economic Life* (Grand Rapids: Wm. B. Eerdmans Publishing Co., 1995).

13. Lee Hardy, *The Fabric of His Design* (Grand Rapids: Wm. B. Eerdmans Publishing Co., 1990), 46.

14. Ibid., 66.

15. Pope John Paul II, *On the Hundredth Anniversary of Rerum Novarum, Centesimus Annus* (Washington, DC: United States Catholic Conference, [May 1] 1991), 83 and 96.

16. Felice Schwartz's proposal for a differentiated career track for women, first espoused in her article on "Management Women and the New Facts of Life" (*Harvard Business Review* 67/1 [Jan./Feb. 1989]: 65), is further explicated in her book, *Breaking With Tradition, Women and Work: The New Facts of Life* (New York: Warner Books, 1992).

17. Robert Bellah, et al., *Habits of the Heart* (Berkeley, CA: Univ. of California Press, 1985).

18. Pope John Paul II, *On the Hundredth Anniversary of Rerum Novarum, Centesimus Annus*.

19. Most standard management textbooks have portions of an introductory chapter devoted to these early classical theorists. One such source is Richard L. Daft's *Management* (New York: Dryden Press, 1988), chapter 2.

20. Elton Mayo was an organizational psychologist employed by the Western Electric Company, charged with improving productivity. The result of his now-famous Hawthorne experiments was the perception that improving human relations in the workplace is the best strategy for increasing productivity.

21. Douglas McGregor, *The Human Side of Enterprise* (New York: McGraw-Hill, 1960).

22. Robert Greenleaf, *Servant Leadership* (New York: Paulist Press, 1977).

23. Joan Acker, "Hierarchies, Jobs, Bodies: A Theory of Gendered Organizations," in Judith Lorber and Susan A. Farrell, *The Social Construction of Gender* (Newbury Park, CA: Sage Publications, 1990); Mary F. Belenky, et al, *Women's Ways of Knowing* (New York: Basic Books, 1986); Patricia Hill Collins, *Black Feminist Thought* (Cambridge, MA: Unwin Hyman, Inc., 1990); Carol Gilligan, *In a Different Voice* (Cambridge, MA: Harvard University Press, 1982).

24. For further descriptions of their leadership theories see James McGregor Burns, *Leadership* (New York: Harper and Row, 1978); Bernard M. Bass, *Leadership and Performance Beyond Expectations* (New York: The Free Press, 1985); Joseph L. Badaracco, Jr., and Richard R. Ellsworth, *Leadership and the Quest for Integrity* (Boston: Harvard Business School Press, 1989).

25. Max DePree, *Leadership is an Art* (New York: Doubleday, 1989); *Leadership Jazz* (New York: Dell Publishing, 1992).

26. This particular definition was taken from the textbook by Richard L. Daft, *Management* (New York: Dryden Press, 1988), 492.

27. A more detailed explanation of shamrock organizations can be found in Charles Handy, *The Age of Unreason* (Boston: Harvard Business School Press, 1989), 87–115.

28. For a further explication of world-formative faith, see Nicholas Wolterstorff, *Until Justice and Peace Embrace* (Grand Rapids: Wm. B. Eerdmans Publishing Co., 1983), 3–22.

29. Cornelius Plantinga, *Not the Way It's Supposed to Be: A Breviary of Sin* (Grand Rapids: Wm. B. Eerdmans Publishing Co., 1995), 10.

30. Wolterstorff, 71.

31. Plantinga, 25.

32. For a fuller explication of the Old Testament concept of Sabbath, see John Schneider, *Godly Materialism* (Downer's Grove, IL: InterVarsity Press, 1994).

33. Stephen R. Covey, *The Seven Habits of Highly Effective People* (New York: Simon and Schuster, 1989), 287–307.

34. For a fuller exegesis of this second aspect of the Old Testament Sabbath and its implications for New Testament times, see "Stewardship, Sabbath and Time," an unpublished paper by Dr. John D. Mason of Gordon College, presented at the Global Stewardship Conference sponsored by the Christianity Today Institute, March 1996.

Notes to Chapter 2

1. "Economic Justice for All," in David J. O'Brien and Thomas A. Shannon, eds., *Catholic Social Thought: The Documentary Heritage* (Maryknoll, NY: Orbis Books, 1992), ¶68.

2. *Sollicitudo Rei Socialis*, in O'Brien and Shannon, ¶38.

3. See Elizabeth Johnson, *She Who Is: The Mystery of God in Feminist Theological Discourse* (New York: Crossroad, 1993).

4. Elisabeth Schüssler Fiorenza, *Jesus: Miriam's Child, Sophia's Prophet; Critical Issues in Feminist Christology* (New York: Continuum, 1994).

5. Mary D. Pellauer, "Moral Callousness and Moral Sensitivity: Violence against Women," in *Women's Consciousness, Women's Conscience: A Reader in Feminist Ethics*, ed. Barbara Hilkert Andolsen, Christine E. Gudorf, and Mary D. Pellauer (San Francisco: Harper & Row, 1985), 33–50.

6. *Good for Business: Making Full Use of the Nation's Human Capital: The Environmental Scan: A Fact-finding Report*, Government Document #L1.2: B96 (Washington, DC: U. S. Department of Labor, 1995).

7. "Women in the Workforce: An Overview," U.S. Department of Labor, Bureau of Labor Statistics Statistics, Report #892 (July 1995), 9.

8. Barbara F. Reskin and Patricia A. Roos, *Job Queues, Gender Queues: Explaining Women's Inroads into Male Occupations* (Philadelphia: Temple University Press, 1990), 309.

9. William Julius Wilson, *When Work Disappears: The World of the New Urban Poor* (New York: Alfred A. Knopf, 1996).

10. Barbara Hilkert Andolsen, *Good Work at the Video Display Terminal: A Feminist Ethical Analysis of Changes in Clerical Work* (Knoxville: University of Tennessee Press, 1989), 34–36.

11. Juliet B. Schor, *The Overworked American: The Unexpected Decline of Leisure* (New York: Basic Books, 1991), 20–21.

12. "Women in the Workforce," 14.

Notes to Chapter 3

1. Florynce R. Kennedy, as quoted in John Brady, "Freelancer with No Time to Write," in *Writer's Digest* (Cincinnati, February 1974).

2. Graef Crystal, *Los Angeles Times*, July 23, 1995, as cited by Elmer W. Johnson, "Corporate Soulcraft in the Age of Brutal Markets" (May 2, 1996; privately circulated), 6. Cf. Robert B. Reich, *The Work of Nations: Preparing Ourselves for 21st-Century Capitalism* (New York: Vintage Books, 1992), 7.

3. Johnson, "Corporate Soulcraft," 6.

4. Nancy Millman, "Still more likely CEO candidates," *Chicago Tribune*, May 26, 1996, section 5, page 1.

5. Reich, esp. 4–5, 9.

6. I here draw extensively on my prior discussions of the professions in *Grounding Professional Ethics in a Pluralistic Society* (New York: Haven Publications, 1983); "On Being a Professional, Morally Speaking," in *Moral Responsibility and the Professions*, ed. Bernard Baumrin and Benjamin Freedman (New York: Haven Publishing Corporation, 1983), 42–61. "Clergy Ethics and the Professional Ethics Model," in *Clergy Ethics in a Changing Society*, ed. James Wind, Russell Burck, Paul Camenisch, and Dennis McCann (Louisville: Westminster/John Knox Press, 1991), 114–133; "The Moral Foundations of Scientific Ethics and Responsibility," *Journal of Dental Research* 75/2 (Feb. 1996): 825–31.

7. For further development of this theme, see Paul F. Camenisch, "Patient Trust in an Age of Institutional Care," written for Lilly/Poynter Center (Indiana University) seminar on "Religion, Morality and the Professions in America" (1995).

Contributors

Shirley J. Roels taught management and served as chair of the Department of Economics and Business before becoming the Dean of Academic Administration at Calvin College. She is also an organizational consultant to the Christian Reformed Church, and has been involved in projects focusing especially on the relationship of faith to economic life in both Russia and China. She is the author (with Richard C. Chewing and John W. Eby) of *Business Through the Eyes of Faith* (HarperCollins, 1990) and a co-editor of *On Moral Business* (Eerdmans, 1995).

Barbara Hilkert Andolsen is Helen Bennett McMurray Professor of Social Ethics at Monmouth University and has served on the editorial boards of the *Journal of Religious Ethics* and *The Annual of the Society of Christian Ethics*. Widely recognized as a religious feminist and advocate for racial and ethnic minorities, she is the author of a number of articles and essays, as well as of *"Daughters of Jefferson, Daughters of Bootblacks": Racism and American Feminism* (Mercer University Press, 1986) and *Good Work at the Video Display Terminal: A Feminist Ethical Analysis of Changes in Clerical Work* (University of Tennessee Press, 1989).

Paul F. Camenisch is Professor and former Chair of the Department of Religious Studies at DePaul University. In addition to consulting with several professional organizations, he has published widely in the field. His books include *Grounding Professional Ethics in a Pluralistic Society* (Haven Publications, 1983); *Clergy Ethics in a Changing Society*, edited with James Wind, Dennis P. McCann, et al. (Westminster/John Knox Press, 1991); and *Religious Methods and Resources in Bioethics* (Kluwer Academic Publishers, 1994), which he edited.

Max L. Stackhouse is Professor of Christian Ethics and Director of the Project on Public Theology at Princeton Theological Seminary.

He is the author of *Public Theology and Political Economy* (University Press of America, 1991), *Creeds, Society and Human Rights* (Eerdmans, 1984; Parthenon, 1996), *Christian Social Ethics in a Global Era* (with Peter L. Berger, Dennis P. McCann, and M. Douglas Meeks; Abingdon, 1995), and the primary editor of *On Moral Business* (Eerdmans, 1995).